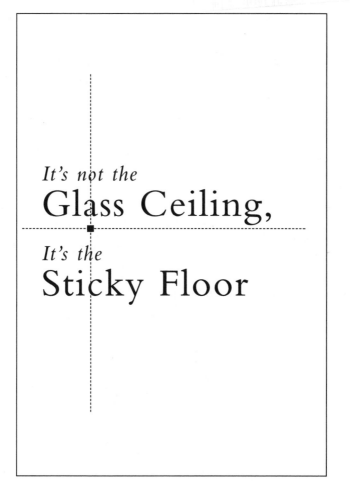

It's not the
Glass Ceiling,
It's the
Sticky Floor

KAREN ENGBERG, M.D.

It's not the
Glass Ceiling,

It's the
Sticky Floor

and Other Things
Our Daughters Should
Know about Marriage, Work,
and Motherhood

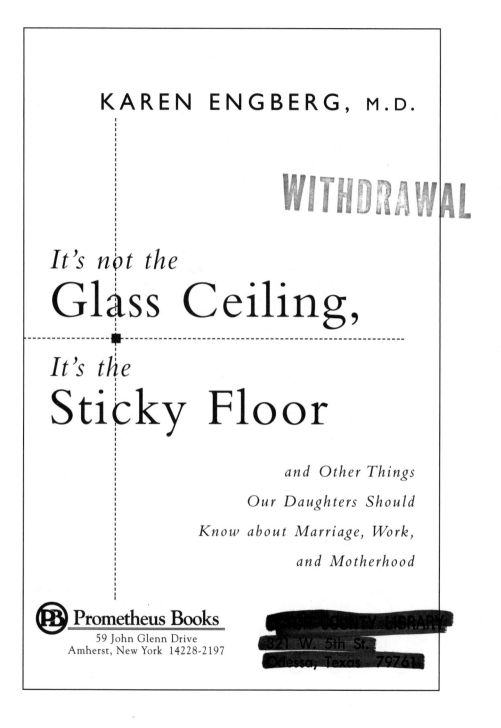 **Prometheus Books**
59 John Glenn Drive
Amherst, New York 14228-2197

Excerpt from *One for the Books—Confessions of a Small-Press Publisher* by John M. Daniel (Fithian Press, 1997) with permission from John M. Daniel, author and publisher.

Excerpt from Barbara Aronstein Black's speech reprinted with her permission.

Published 1999 by Prometheus Books

Inquiries should be addressed to
Prometheus Books, 59 John Glenn Drive, Amherst, New York 14228–2197.
VOICE: 716–691–0133, ext. 207.
FAX: 716–564–2711.
WWW.PROMETHEUSBOOKS.COM

03 02 01 00 99   5 4 3 2 1

Library of Congress Cataloging-in-Publication Data

Engberg, Karen.
    It's not the glass ceiling, it's the sticky floor : and other things our daughters should know about marriage, work, and motherhood / Karen Engberg.
        p.   cm.
    ISBN 1–57392–745–7 (cloth : alk. paper)
    1. Marriage. 2. Motherhood. 3. Working mothers. 4. Work and family.
5. Parenthood. 6. Mothers and daughters. 7. Stress (Psychology) I. Title.
HQ734 .E65   1999
306.874'3—dc21   98–17668
                                                                                    CIP

Printed in the United States of America on acid-free paper

This one is for my mother, Kay Engberg,
for a lifetime of encouragement, patience, wisdom,
and an ability to understand what really matters.

Contents

Acknowledgments

Where to start? The impetus for this book came from a variety of both likely and unlikely sources, all of which and whom contributed in some way to a long and fortunate process that goes back fifteen years.

Had it not been for the indefatigable encouragement and counsel of my good friend, confidante, colleague, and cohort in motherhood, Pamela McLean, this book might never have been picked up from where it was put down a number of times along the way. I am ever so grateful to Pam, not only for much immediate insight and inspiration, but for years of give-and-take about the topics that inform this book.

Every author needs a sounding board, and I was lucky enough to have several. Many thanks to Amy Bossen, Nanette Boyer, Anne Fisher, Sandy Seale, Judith Loftus, and my sisters, Kristin James, Elizabeth Engberg, and Sallysue Stein for their words of wisdom about the territory women with children and ambitions inhabit, and for their willingness to drop everything to discuss my question of the moment or to read and comment on the material as it came along.

I owe my ability to proceed with this project to a number of individuals who like my writing enough to convince me to keep at it. Linda Bowen deserves a large thank-you for enlisting me to write a weekly column seven years ago. I am also grateful to Melinda Johnson at the *Santa Barbara Press-News* who, while being a continuing source of deadline pressure, is also a font of good humor and ideas.

I'd also like to thank Ron Patel at the *Philadelphia Inquirer* for being willing to try something different six years ago with my "Healthy Kids" column that mixed medicine and motherhood, and all the editors I've worked with at that paper, especially Jane Eisner and Joseph Gamberdello.

I deeply appreciate the influence of Virginia Moran, who suggested the book; Janean Selkirk, who provided the sort of encouragement and guidance that precluded my doing anything but going forth; and Sarah Fenstermaker, who did favors above and beyond the call of friendship by taking her professorial red pen to the margins of the original proposal.

My parents, Kay and Ed Engberg, have been behind this project all the way. My father, as always, was both cheering section and technical/grammar consultant extraordinaire. My mother gave me her example. She taught me what it takes to be a really good mother; the only problem was that in being so good and gracious a mom, she made the job look easier than it usually is.

A word of thanks to my loyal newspaper audience, who have been a wellspring of support, especially those who kept pressing me to write a book and the lady who drives up alongside my car at red lights from time to time to give me a thumbs-up about my latest column.

Finally, I am particularly grateful to my husband, Douglas Jackson, for being able and willing to reconfigure his expectations about marrying a medical colleague to accommodate the realities of raising a family. He has been no less surprised by it all than I. And—is "thank you" the right term?—to the best, craziest, funniest, but most relentlessly demanding teachers I will ever have, my four children: Vanessa, Madeleine, Galen, and Francesca.

Introduction

My thirteen-year-old daughter recently completed an autobiography, an assignment in which she was to illustrate and describe her past and present, then imagine her future. It wasn't the contents that pulled my thoughts aside as much as the dedication that read, "To all the people who have said to me / I can be anything I want to be." This sky's-the-limit advice was precisely what I grew up with and has served me well. I've found, however, that because our culture, if not our biology, still operates differently for men than for women, this notion is never as simple for women as it is for men. This, in my experience, has less to do with cultural gender biases than it does with all the nitty-gritty details of life that aren't ordinarily discussed in polite company. What gets in the way for women, in other words, is not the glass ceiling, but the sticky floor.

Reading my daughter's life story made me think about the twists and turns in my own life and how, back in my early twenties, I boarded a train for one destination in life and ended up at quite another. As a junior in college majoring in American history with a plan to pursue journalism, I developed a fascination with the field of medicine and set about becoming a physician.

The ticket was costly and the trip lengthy, but the satisfaction was immeasurable. Then, just as the train was pulling into the station, just as I was arriving at my M.D. degree, I had my first child. It wasn't long before it became apparent that I was no longer on the express train to a glorious career in medicine, but on one with many more stops at unpredictable stations and with an unforeseeable destination. I was on the train called Motherhood.

The underpinning for my initial confidence in becoming a physician came from growing up with the women's movement. All the career doors had been thrown open and anything was possible. It was a heady feeling to be a torchbearer and on my way to an exciting profession. Not a single obstacle seemed to stand between me and what my mother could never have imagined for herself. Oh sure, medical school was expensive, and there was the matter of the years it would take, and some real naysayers warned that medicine was a bastion of male chauvinism. But these, to anyone of the feminist persuasion who was smitten with medicine, like myself, were just details, minor nuisances, and nothing significant in the way of deterrents.

The real obstacles, it later became apparent, weren't being talked about at all, not by any nefarious design, but because this particular social experiment had never been done on a grand scale. My generation represented the first large number of test tubes into which was stirred one part career, one part marriage, and one or more parts motherhood. The results of the assay were not obvious for many years; only then did it become apparent that some of the ingredients didn't mix as smoothly as everyone had assumed they would.

Several dilemmas emerged from this experiment, most of them still begging for answers. I wonder now, as I never would have when I first blithely boarded that train, who is supposed to take care of the children when parents are all on their way to some other destination besides home. I ponder how to advise my daughters because, unlike my mother who had no way of knowing how caring for a family would combine with pursuing a career, I have had the reality check of doing just that. I ask myself what a family is when none of the members have time to be a family. And I think wishfully of a time ahead when the majority of men will come to better know and share the tasks and rewards of being at home.

My mother couldn't have predicted the quandary into which my generation has wandered, but I have no such excuse not to tell my daughters what I know. Rather than have them come to me years from now and ask, as they are straddling an uncomfortable chasm between fast-paced careers and sane home lives, "How come you never told us it would be like this?" I want to say it now. I want them to know that, while it may not be as simple as they suppose, they are lucky to be women, and there are more ways than those they might initially imagine in which they can be—of course—anything they want to be.

—Karen Engberg, M.D.

Chapter One

She Who Is Ready to Face Life Alone Is Ready to Get Married

One is not born a woman, one becomes one.
—Simone de Beauvoir

The process of coming of age has changed tremendously for women during the past half century. Women are living longer in better health, have an extensive choice of careers, are bearing children over a greater span of years, and have long, productive intervals after their children are grown. This seeming freedom, however, has not come without added expectations: schooling has been extended to regularly include college and commonly graduate school; women are expected to participate in breadwinning and money management; and given the current technology, women are now called upon as never before to control their reproductive destinies. Because the transitions and decisions a young woman makes during her late teens and twenties will so greatly influence what comes later, it is essential that these years be negotiated with patience, awareness, determination, and self-discipline. The resulting self-sufficient woman will not only live longer with more choices, but be happier doing so.

17

Take Time to Make Time

Like most other professional women I know, I came of age with the women's movement. At least this is what I thought until I looked back sometime later and realized that coming of age takes a good deal longer than we tend to think it does, especially while we're in the midst of it. As it turned out, this reality held true not just for me, but for the women's movement as well.

It's a peculiarity of our culture that we talk about "growing up" as some sort of concrete process that begins at birth and ends when we move out of our parents' home, graduate from college, or, at the very latest and regardless of when it happens, get married. Growing up, however, as anyone who thinks they have done it will attest, is a much more protracted—and painful—experience than just arriving at an age when you can drive, go to college, drink liquor, be drafted, vote, get married, or have kids, not necessarily in that order. Our culture hangs its hat, not to mention its democracy and car keys, on arbitrarily designated ages, and creates legal and cultural taboos about doing certain things or behaving in certain ways before those ages. This age thermostat is set low, however, too often reflecting a convenient more than an ideal situation.

This coming-of-age business is complicated, nowadays perhaps even more so than when I was navigating it. First, for young women, come the physical and emotional changes of puberty which then distract from all other developmental tasks for years to come. Bemoaning the arrival of her period one day, one of my daughters at age twelve repined, "This isn't fair. Why do girls need to have periods before they're going to have babies, anyway? When we're responsible adults, like maybe twenty-one, would be soon enough."

Her sentiment is not uncommon or difficult to understand. Just when a girl is making the break from the nice, safe, predictable routines of elementary school to the social soup of junior high, her periods begin, her breasts grow—or don't—and her body takes on dimensions uncomfortably referable to her mother. Her friends become her raison d'être, her parents become utensils to use only when absolutely necessary, and boys—the very same ones she has taken for granted for years—become enigmatically indispensable. In the midst of this she's expected to pay attention in algebra and become progressively more responsible. By the time high school is underway, some naive version of adulthood and all those heretofore taboos beckon enticingly. So, too, do an array of real choices that can be at once exhilarating and immobilizing. What happens at this time of a young woman's life—the identity she chooses and begins to move toward and the degree to which she is helped to maintain her emotional well-being—can have enormous repercussions on her future.

This is where the coming-of-age plot thickens. It's not, after all, as though a person in her late teens sits down and just picks an identity and then systematically sets out to aspire to it. Rather, an accumulation of experiences begins to crystallize, ever so gradually, into an identity trend. I remember with painful clarity trying out the too-smart-to-touch image, the preppy look, the hippie persona, the mod mode, and the beer-drinking buddy role, sometimes dressing one role and acting another. Eventually I scavenged the most useful elements of each of these, rolled them into an ambition to do something with my life, and went forth to educate myself accordingly. But this took a long time. Intellect and image tripped over each other regularly throughout college and medical school, indeed until I was well into my late twenties. Was I supposed to be smart or sexy? Could I be both?

Many a well-adjusted adult woman has a hard time with these issues; younger women can only hope to sort them out slowly but surely. Myriad conflicting messages conspire to make this an uphill search and one laden with land mines. The question, "What do men want?" gets placed alongside the question, "What do I want?" and creates moments of pure, unmitigated befuddlement until experience begins to provide clarity. There are times, even in the midst of a one-tracked pursuit of a goal, when the only thing a young woman may know for sure is that she can get married and have children. Yet only when a woman has lived happily alone, identified and made substantial headway toward her ambitions, and pretty thoroughly surveyed the landscape of male partners is she "ready" to think about marriage.

We refer to getting married as settling down because it has a way of taking the tumult out of our search for meaning and self-knowledge—at least temporarily. Vowing to another person that you will be an altruistic and mature person makes you become that, happily or unhappily, for a while anyway. It also has a way of making you stop where you are from a developmental standpoint. Trying to be who you are supposed to be for this person you married can throw a wet blanket on the pursuit of individuation; you end up following someone else's shoulds instead of your own coulds. Had I gotten married in my late teens (cringe), I would have chosen a hippie guy and been a hippie mom, unless some significant experience had snapped me out of it. Had I gotten married in my early twenties, I might not have gone to medical or graduate school at all, but settled into figuring out what it meant to be a wife and helping make ends meet in a nonprofessional capacity. Even in my midtwenties, although I was chugging along at a good clip with specific goals firmly in mind, self-knowledge was at a premium.

Although marrying young challenges the odds against long-term stability, it doesn't have to be a self-fulfilling tragedy. In the absence of children, you can scavenge considerable wisdom from marriage to apply further down the road to your hopes and dreams, whether or not you still travel this road with the same partner. But marriage at any age has a way of making procreation permissible, and because children need stability and emotionally well-formed parents in order to pursue their own individuation, it's the kids to whom misfortune inevitably accrues in premature marriages.

Revisiting this often treacherous coming-of-age period with my daughters, this time as a sideline observer, makes me a little nervous. The discovery zone between high school and the late twenties is laden with a frightful number of choices and learning experiences, the most effective of which are inevitably painful: sex; love; intellectual and physical accomplishment; and the task of moving toward a marital partnership, a career, and, perhaps, motherhood. It's a long, essential process requiring seemingly endless postponements of gratification.

By the time she gets to what she now sees as the magical adult age of twenty-one, I'm guessing—I'm hoping—my daughter will have taken the marker representing her notion of when marriage and babies might be a good idea and moved it up a few notches closer to thirty. Moreover, I hope she never sees marriage or children as a finish line, but as an ongoing endeavor, remembering along the way that life is both long and short, and that living in each moment is the best way to effectively garner what's needed for the next.

Seek—Whatever That Means—and You Shall Find

Inseparable from coming of age is deciding what you want to do with your life. Some people know from a very early age exactly what they want to be when they "grow up" and systematically work toward that goal. More power to them. Many others muddle along in the general direction of some vague purpose and make up something clever to say when their parents' friends ask, "So, what are your plans?" It's pretty scary to have a lifestyle in mind and face a bunch of adults with a sequence of events planned for you when you haven't the faintest notion of what you want to do or how to support yourself while you're making up your mind. Figuring the whole thing out can be less a self-willed determination than a gradually progressive, if hodgepodge, pursuit.

This is born out in the biographies of many accomplished women. In her poignant autobiography, *The Road from Coorain* (Vintage Books, 1989), Jill Ker Conway traces the winding path she followed to education and career. Leaving high school provoked the following observation: "I tried hard to develop the right aspirations, but had no map of the future to guide me. I remembered my father's advice about what to do if I were ever to become lost in the bush. 'Don't panic and rush about,' he said. 'Stay in the shade and wait for the night sky. You'll be able to see the Southern Cross, and you can navigate by that.'" After a brief stint at the University of Sydney, Conway dropped out, then took a job in a doctor's office until the novelty wore off. When she again returned to the university, she discovered an affinity and passion for history and literature. This focus served her well thereafter, helping her overcome the personal bonds of a needy mother and the confining gender bias of Australia's academic world. Eventually she left Australia for America, where she became the first woman president of Smith College.

Lots of other highly accomplished women tell similar stories of coming and going academically, of landing jobs here and there, of trying a little of this or that before discovering a direction. Christine Todd Whitman, New Jersey's first woman governor, had an up-and-down experience with her education, pulling out of elementary school in Europe, changing high schools in search of a good fit, and finally having her passion for politics motivate her through college. She knew what she wanted but wasn't wild about the educational dues she had to pay to get there.

Then there is Rosie O'Donnell, who flunked out of two colleges before launching her wildly successful career as an actor and comedian. The arena of artistic endeavor is, in fact, filled with women who had to get beyond cultural or family expectations, social or psychological handicaps, or chemical dependencies before finding their passions.

The best advice I ever heard—which wasn't advice so much as an observation to live by—came from Margaret Bourke-White, the renowned photographer whose work constituted the first cover of *Life* magazine back in the 1930s. "Work," went her little pearl of wisdom, "is something you can count on, a trusted lifelong friend who never deserts you." The caveat to this, however, is that this "friend" isn't always something you can set out to find but one that often has to find you.

Finding or being found by that friend for life called work is a curious course that has been ritualized in our culture despite evidence pointing to its serendipitous nature. In ironic contrast to the usual course of events, for instance, much ado is made about preparing for and selecting just the right college, and this before high school even begins to wind down. Kids who are at least as and usually more interested in how to sneak out of the house at night without being found out by their parents as they are in higher education are expected to develop a sense of urgency about their futures. They can get stalled by what others expect of them rather than thriving on the possibilities at hand.

It reminds me a little of parents' tendencies to be ready for their three- or four-year-olds to read years before the kids are ready. Every once in a while a four-year-old will read. But with reading—as with college and career selection—it's more often layers of preparation combined with a developmental readiness that gives way to a competence, not someone else's timetable. When it becomes important to the kid, and when she has enough information to do so, she reads—or decides what to do with her life.

Despite the overarching importance of keeping as many doors open as possible during the late teens and early twenties, the first thing you're asked to do after selecting a college is to declare a major. Some students take this so seriously as to irrevocably cast themselves in a particular role from the time they first lug a suitcase over the threshold of a dorm room as freshmen. Most, however, change that major several times along the way in testimony to the absence of predestination when it comes to career choices. They add to the usual four years whatever time is necessary to get passionate—whether advertently or inadvertently—about their futures, then just when all funding has dried up or their credibility with the registrar or their parents is in serious jeopardy they finally say, "I've got it!" and get serious.

Often, however, it's not the college major, the funding, or any deadlines that nudge or propel a career direction, but a part-time job or extraneous circumstance. Timing, a factor over which we have virtually no control, is frequently the baton that conducts the next several years or even decades. Author John M. Daniel describes this phenomenon in his memoir, *One for the Books: Confessions of a Small Press Publisher* (Fithian Press, 1997):

> I became an English major pretty much automatically. Having no choice was a pattern for me, although I didn't recognize it at the time. After all, I was just at college because that's what a young person did after high school (or prep school). To the degree that I rebelled at all in that rebellious time of life, it was by choosing to go to Stanford instead of Yale. I chose Stanford because four winters in New England were enough for me, and because I too had read Kerouac and had decided there was something magical about California, although that probably had more to do with Doris Day.
>
> I chose English because my brother Neil had also taught me to juggle and yodel and drive; it was natural that I should follow in his footsteps. . . .

My own experience leading up to college was not much different. My teen rebellion took the form of declaring that I wasn't going to attend college at all. Then, after a stint as a waitress and another as a bank teller, the reasons my parents had wished college upon me became crystal clear. At the moment the novelty of handling everyone else's money but my own and riding a bike to work in the rain wore thin, I had missed the application deadline for just about every eastern college except Boston University, to which I hastily applied. I was accepted and immediately headed across the country to a school about which I knew virtually nothing and for no other reason than it had been more deadline-friendly than my other options.

The accidental nature of the search for purpose and place often persists beyond college. If you ask my husband why he became a physician, he'll tell you that in 1970, the year he graduated from college with a degree in electrical engineering, the Vietnam War was at full tilt. History and his graduation intersected at a moment when only two graduate courses of study qualified young men for draft deferments: divinity and medicine. He chose the latter and became a doctor, not because of any burning altruistic interest, but because it seemed the most appealing of his three choices. It turned out to be an excellent choice.

While all this seems like a frightfully haphazard way of coming to terms with that which is to ultimately be your means of survival, it is more likely, not less, the case now than when I was contemplating my options. Despite the emerging women's movement, a fair number of women still went to college in those days with the primary intent of finding a husband. The rest of us sat through courses with no future applicability beyond that of fanning the flames of feminine ambition, courses like Women in American History, Heroines of the Twentieth Century, and The Feminist Identity. We revered the young, humorless professors with streaked hair, miniskirts, black turtlenecks, and dark tights who, while taking themselves very seriously and dragging on Virginia Slims during class, asked us, their confused students, to contemplate the larger meaning of meager events.

College women no longer have to convince themselves or anyone else that they've come a long way, and fewer put in their four years just to find the right guy. If in the 1970s John Daniel was at college "because that's what a young person did after high school," it's even more true now. Graduate school is nearly to college nowadays what college was to high school thirty years ago. College and even grad school are just what young people do, some with a definite eye toward the future and some just following a Peter Pan approach to the harsh realities of growing up.

For those who stand to inherit a family business or have a generations-long legacy in a given profession to honor, the soul-search preliminary to a career choice might be a no-brainer. Family history may beckon them compellingly to teach, counsel, invent, write, act, or make airplane-tray tables. Some may also feel trapped by their family's past, but rebellion—my modus—then supplies a direction all its own. Most people coming out of college, however, have no choice but to take their genetic endowments, add to these what experience and inclination have to offer, hope that serendipity is on their side, and either go out into the world or apply to graduate school.

College and graduate educations notwithstanding, the primordial ooze of influences that colors a career search includes everything from playing first chair in the school orchestra to flushing a goldfish, and from being a middle child to taking first prize in a science fair. The resulting rock star, veterinarian, lawyer, or physics professor may not be able to identify the source of her inspiration when she looks back. A long, often curious list of variables comes to bear on what a person will list in the "occupation" blank on applications and forms in her adult life. Some of these decisions and choices are consciously determined; many others are subconscious or at least not formally recognized motivators.

Published material on how to choose a career is legion. The process—whether you have a high school diploma or a Ph.D.—has been wrested from one of a soul search to that given up by charts, tests, computer analyses, self-help schemes, personality profiles, how-to-be-interviewed theories, and counseling centers. Juxtaposed with this systematic approach is the current career credo that advises that you follow your heart, go after your dreams, pick a parachute color, and never take no for an answer. The eventual dilemma for a few men but for a vast number of women is that the heart, the dream, the parachute color, and the answers may change more times than a college major in the course of having children and raising a family. Understanding this—what some would call the dirty little secret of the women's movement—can only help future generations of women seek their futures more realistically and be happier with what they find.

Save Your Strength

I'm no expert on money, but this is one topic over which you can have some control. And while this issue will affect you as surely and as extensively as the career or mate you choose, it is one about which many women remain passive their whole lives. A little like taking that calcium supplement during your teens to protect your bones two decades hence, keeping a prospective eye on your finances will protect numerous aspects of your life and permit choices you wouldn't otherwise have. Unfortunately, again like that calcium, financial planning is easy to put off indefinitely.

Whether you earn small or large amounts of money is not as relevant as what you do with those bucks. Any financial expert will tell you that even small numbers of dollars can generate handsome returns when invested over time. That means the money you make when you are young with few financial responsibilities (no mortgage or children) can make your life a lot more comfortable as things get more complicated if—and this is the big if—you have the discipline to invest some amount of it sooner rather than later.

The obstacle to such investing is most often a lack of knowledge about how to proceed. Passbook savings accounts, into which a lot of money is placed for lack of money moxie, will end up eroding the value of your money over time, even when inflation is at its lowest. If your money is earning 2 or 3 percent in a savings account, a 3 percent inflation rate will barely maintain or possibly even reduce the value of your savings. It's tempting, as you watch the absolute amount of money grow with sequential deposits, to feel pleased with this progress and pat yourself on the back about it. In reality, however, you might almost as well stash this money in an envelope and tape it to the underside of a drawer the way my grandmother used to do decades ago. Yes, your money will be there the next time you look, but it will not be working for you the way it could.

To put myself through medical school in the early 1980s, I had to choose between committing to four years of postresidency military service in exchange for tuition and living expenses, or borrowing the money. I chose the latter course because I wanted to keep my options open, and proceeded to apply for two different types of student loans with annual interest rates of 3 percent and 7 percent. These funded at the beginning of each semester, and after paying my tuition I always had a sum of money left to cover other expenses over the ensuing several months. During these years, a 5 percent annual rate of inflation added to the interest on the loans to far exceed the 4 percent interest being paid on passbook savings accounts. Even though my money didn't stay in one place for long periods of time, I was still experiencing a net erosion of my banked money.

At the same time, interest on money market accounts, even those with only six-month minimum deposit requirements, was about 13 percent. It wasn't until one of my more financially savvy classmates pointed this out that I realized the place to stash my loan money was not in the old familiar passbook account, but in a money market fund where it would keep pace with inflation and the loan's annual cost, and even accrue a little interest during the short time it lasted.

One of the things that becomes impressive about our compulsory education system as you begin to call upon it for guidance is the glaring holes it continues to embrace. One of these oversights is the lack of instruction provided on a topic as important as money management. A college economics course or two is the extent of many people's formal education about money. Yet an abstract notion about goods and services won't do the trick when it comes to paying for your kid's tuition— preschool, then before you know it, college—or filling the gaps in a retirement plan.

Some fortunate individuals hail from families with financial wherewithal and come into adulthood from traditions of good money-management practices. But most of us have to take the initiative, do our homework, and learn from our mistakes. Like exercise, exploring options for investment is often more compelling when it has a social aspect. Especially for anyone who feels lost on the subject, an investment group or a network of friends with similar investment goals can up the ante, maximize the satisfaction, and decrease the work involved in getting the financial wizard in yourself up and running.

The specifics of how to invest well and plan for financial security are beyond the scope of this book; authorities have written about this subject well. Just getting cozy with the terminology may be where you want to start, after which you'll need a daily newspaper with a reputable business or financial section. Then a facilitator with experience setting up investment groups can help you avoid time-consuming or costly mistakes. You can also get on the Internet and become familiar with what investment instruction the various on-line services offer.

However you decide to proceed, you should start sooner, not later. Waiting for the "right time" to begin putting away money will take you directly to middle age or further without ever passing Go to collect your dividends. Most money managers will tell you that investing over the long haul—twenty years and more—is the best way to maximize your return.

That means starting now. (Well, maybe not right now, but as soon as you're done reading this book.) Don't wait until you have a large sum to invest; it probably won't happen. In the meantime, the small sums you systematically invest will be on their way to becoming a large sum.

Clearing the financial fog and being savvy about money before you enter a partnership will allow you to operate from a position of strength. Gone are the days when women should have to ask their spouse for money, even if he is the sole breadwinner in the partnership. The feminists of the sixties and seventies noted knowingly that money and power are often synonymous. The truth in this wisdom will become increasingly apparent as you negotiate your way through both personal and business relationships. You will want—who wouldn't—a sufficient share of the power in any partnership to have things benefit you. Learning to acquire and manage money wisely is the first step toward this goal. Begin early to save your strength.

Look Past the Pecs, Listen Past the Promises

I was sitting at dinner one evening with several couples, all of whom had been married for at least ten years. The banter, as it often does in situations like this, moved to a not-so-subtle, albeit lighthearted, commentary about how the woman in each couple differed from the man.

"He's a neat freak, and I'm totally disorganized," one woman remarked.

"Yeah," sighed another. "He lives for ESPN, and I just want the television out of my house."

"How about popcorn?" asked a third woman. "It's bad enough we can hardly ever agree on a movie we both want to see, but then when we finally do, he wants to share the popcorn. Ever try to make popcorn last through the movie when someone is scarfing it by the handful? I'm telling you, sharing popcorn is hard on a marriage."

Finally, a fourth woman in the group looked at her husband and smiled. "I read this caption on a cartoon in the newspaper this morning. It said, 'This would be a perfect relationship if it wasn't for you.' We had a good laugh about that because I think we basically both believe it."

This is the sort of talk—reflecting that not only are men and women different but that a sense of humor is indispensable to a relationship—that people who have been married for a few years take for granted. It makes light of the notion that the "perfect" relationship exists. Younger people can be made uncomfortable by such talk, however, and invariably think to themselves, "I won't ever feel that way; I won't even joke about it. I'll always be simpatico with my mate. I would *never* just stay with someone for the sake of the children." Yet most married couples who stay together do so for reasons that have nothing to do with why they got together in the first place. Although the basic personality traits and background each person brings to the marital equation are crucial to enabling good results, adult development doesn't reside on a plateau (for long, anyway). Because individuals continue to grow and change and learn, new reasons for moving forward with a partner inevitably replace the old reasons. Sometimes this is pretty and sometimes it's not.

The natural history of a marriage, what happens to it over time, depends on innumerable factors, most of which can't be predicted in advance. Births, deaths, hirings, firings, health, illness, and myriad unforeseen events take their toll, singly, collectively, and irretrievably as anniversaries accrue. The most important component of a durable marriage has to do with the basic compatibility of the two people involved—not even passionate love so much as mutual respect, the determination (and capacity) to be happy, and a willingness to compromise. These things need to be in place right up front. Hair styles, jobs, food preferences—all the extraneous factors—may change numerous times during a marriage, but the fundamental components of personality and basic compatibility are much less amenable to change. If an undercurrent of emotional discomfort or incompatibility exists before marriage, the ceremony won't make it go away and will usually only exacerbate the chinks.

One of the first things a psychologist does in assessing the status of a marriage or a couple is to determine whether it's a good match or a mismatch. The latter often results from a premature marriage, an inability to reckon with what is right in front of their eyes before tying the knot, or a fundamentally incompatible view of how the world works. And while all of these concerns sound predictable and therefore avoidable, it's a fact of life—as surely as any bird or bee—that mismatched marriages abound.

So how do you "find" a good match in the era beyond arranged marriages? Despite the temptation to believe in the gospel according to Hollywood, which suggests in movies like *Sleepless in Seattle* that a single perfect mate is out there for the finding, history indicates that trusting your intelligence, intuition, and past experience is the best way to arrange your own marital happiness. Once again, as in discovering a career, serendipity is the deus ex machina within this context.

Intelligence, or thinking things through, does play a role in the mating process. Conventional wisdom has now arrived at the pretty compelling conclusion that men and women are different. (When I say "now," I mean as opposed to twenty years ago, when the differences between men and women were generally thought to be more a matter of nurture than nature.) This conclusion derives from several parts science and research, and several parts observation by the pig-in-the-python generation* of baby boomer parents who have watched in awe as their baby boys followed markedly different behavioral vectors from birth than did their baby girls. Boys and men, most now agree, are put in motion by brain chemistry and resulting hormonal direction that differ fundamentally from that of girls and women. The discussion has conceded that *vive la différence* is moot and has moved on to a debate about how "opposite" sexes not only survive one another but preferably enjoy the ride. Despite the enlightenment, conduct remains at issue.

For young women growing up in a social milieu that, at least in theory, denies them nothing, being told to be good girls may sound anachronistically laughable or offensive. Surely we haven't come all this way in the battle for parity to be told that we still have to mind our manners around the boys. How about making the guys toe the behavioral line and, for a refreshing change, letting girls be girls. This is a lovely thought that no forward-thinking woman—feminist, postfeminist, or otherwise— could reasonably dispute. Yet while lovely thoughts may have allowed Wendy to fly to Neverland, we earthling women are constrained to having to grow up in the real world. And in the real world women are still sexually harassed, accosted, molested, and brutalized every day by men who have the physical wherewithal to behave badly, often facilitated—not justified but facilitated—by their victim's naïveté.

---

*An adult development term to refer to the demographic swelling consisting of the baby boomer parents.

An insightful mother of four boys, all delightful young fellows now in their twenties, told me one day that raising her boys through their teen years was her greatest challenge. From about age fourteen on, she said, pretty much all they think about is sex. Their female peers flirt and dress provocatively and behave alluringly, but they don't have a clue how this affects the guys. Of the young women, she said, "They don't know what they're doing, who they're dealing with, what they're asking for." The brain chemistry gap prevails from the get go with young women wanting companionship, understanding, and intimacy. Physical and sexual interactions, for women, are a means to accomplishing this goal. For guys, meanwhile, the situation is reversed; concessions to intimacy are the means to sexual interaction, which is, at some often not-so-subtle level, their goal.

That heart and head don't always see eye to eye is the source of inspiration for many a tragic love story, not to mention heated debate among women about whether the head or the heart is the best source of advice. Heart and head, of course, don't have to be mutually exclusive advisors, provided that what the head has to say is not blown off by the heart. Once a woman comes to terms with the fact that what she's after and thinks she's going to get may not be entirely available, especially in the long run, the necessary compromises may be easier to strike. After all, no male partner gets exactly what he wants either, regardless of how good the match.

The dictates of forethought in striking a good marriage (or at least avoiding a precipitous or unfortunate commitment) include living alone and being independent before facing the dependence inherent in every marriage. Being honest is another. It's possible to convince yourself that a significant discrepancy in age, income, race, character, religion, or education between yourself and a partner won't matter because another agenda—loneliness, a surging libido, a ticking biological clock, the desire for financial security, or physical attraction—supersedes, at least for the moment, objective assessment. It's not that discrepancies can't be worked into a good marriage when they are seen for what they are, it's that most couples downplay the differences and pretend they won't matter when they surely will.

Another form of denial involves convincing oneself that love will find a way, that a partner's bad habits and annoying traits will be amenable to the romantic charm of marriage. Those who take this approach soon find out how unromantic marriage can be. The most fruitful way to lend objectivity to the lens through which you regard a prospective mate (or even a regular date) is to ferret out those annoyances and differences and hold them up to the light. That, and not rushing into anything.

This idea of not rushing into anything harkens back to letting yourself come richly of age and know what you want before becoming a partner for life. It also lets you try out various relationships and, if you are willing to look, see the weak spots or self-defeating patterns in your interactions with men. It gives you the luxury of time while you are young, if you are willing to take advantage of it, to make mistakes and change your mind.

The heart, however, can't be kept at bay forever, and sooner or later it will play havoc with objectivity. The urgency women experience about procreating is—at least during their twenties—an irrational but compelling example of this phenomenon. The biological clock ticking deafeningly and blocking out the sound of reason has, from an evolutionary standpoint, guaranteed the survival of the species. Nonetheless, from the standpoint of the impending millennium and the science of reproduction, fertility panic is irrational. When sixty-three-year-old women can become pregnant and deliver babies, little need exists for twenty-five-year-olds to mindlessly respond to their biological clock alarms.

Marriage is one of the most unnatural arrangements imaginable. You spend the most important and perspective-forming years of your life being shaped by a family. Then, just when you have begun to emerge as distinct from that family, you're expected to cast your lot with someone not only of the opposite sex, but from an altogether different family. You're supposed to do this and never look back, to spend the next fifty or sixty years with this person. Never mind that fate doesn't stop dealing cards at this point or suspend a person in the psycho–social–sexual dimension they inhabit when they make this commitment. No, the cards keep coming and after only a few rounds, you may be holding a hand that bears little resemblance to the one you initially agreed to play. You've gotta love something about the game to stick with it.

One way to get an idea of what kind of hand the other person holds is to take a look at his background. A friend, a very bright, accomplished woman, once puzzled aloud about a lawyer she had been dating. She wasn't attracted to him in the least—no "heat," she said—and couldn't figure out why someone as staid as this fellow would be interested in someone as even mildly racy as herself. "I find myself ordering Jack Daniel's on the rocks just to watch his eyebrows go up," she observed. "He doesn't drink at all. I can't figure out why he keeps asking me out."

I asked her what she knew about his upbringing. She related, matter-of-factly, that back in the sixties his mother had been a high profile, fast-lane editor with numerous Hollywood connections. His father had been a conservative, responsible businessman who, until his death, doted on the mother. This one didn't take much figuring. Although there were surely several reasons for the attraction, this man obviously found my friend's moxie reminiscent of his mother's. Yet my friend hadn't even begun to put this two and two together. When I suggested that she looked like home to him, her eyes opened wide. "Of course," she said. "How could I have missed that?"

Yet we all miss some of the most obvious handwriting on the wall when we choose a mate, simply because the initial stages of romantic involvement can be stupefying—I know they were for me—and because we're not taught how to make some of the most important decisions of our lives. We are, by virtue of being inundated with television scenarios and movie plots, taught to ignore the obvious and trust in happy endings. Yet marriage is a beginning, a beginning of a long process of growth and change and not an ending, happy or otherwise.

Such growing and changing can challenge even good marriages. Consider the woman whose father smoked and who marries a smoker (he reminds her of Dad), then decides, perhaps when her father dies or when she becomes pregnant, that smoking is not only toxic but obnoxious. Her husband, somewhat bewildered because, after all, he hasn't done anything different, gets defensive about his position and digs in his heels. "You knew I smoked when you married me," he says. "So what's the problem?" The problem, of course, is that the woman has changed her mind, perhaps become more educated, about smoking. The challenge to both partners is to move forward together as the rules change—which they will, frequently. This capacity to move forward will depend on each partner's ability and willingness to accommodate the other person in reasonable ways. But being reasonable is, of course, a variable function of background and worldview, which is why mismatched couples are seldom able to resolve anything, let alone their differences. Any discussion will follow the vicious cycle of basic incompatibility.

Marriage is a mutual dependency, preferably a felicitous one. When things are going well, no matter how independent you tend to be, relying on someone else and having them rely on you is pretty easy. How a couple negotiates the tough times is the telling point of a marriage. Maybe the best you can do ahead of time is to assess how a prospective partner behaves when, before marriage, the courtship hits bumps. In doing this, pay less attention to the words and appearances of the relationship than to the background music; listen closely to that music. If you feel like the enemy every time a disagreement intervenes; if you observe anger out of proportion to the issue at hand; if you feel pressured to perform sexually; if you ever feel like a second-class citizen in the relationship; or if you feel controlled, demeaned, or even put on a pedestal, understand these things as red flags. If you feel wrung out over premarital adversities, however small and regardless of whether apologies are forthcoming, you can be certain it will only get worse within the context of a marriage.

I once interviewed a baby-sitter who said she wanted the job because she was looking for a nice family to make her happy. I wound up the interview quickly at that point, knowing she wasn't going to be the one for my kids. I was looking for someone who would bring an innate joie de vivre to the position, not expect me and my kids to make her content. Making a good marital match is much the same. It depends on both partners to bring an emotional competence and optimism to the commitment, not on an arrangement in which one or the other of the partners hopes the other person will supply the happiness. The idea is for both partners to be able to say to each other, year after year and regardless of whether they decide to share their popcorn, "This may not be a perfect relationship, but it is pretty darn good because of you."

Refuse to Be Intimidated

The subject of domestic violence was dragged out of our national closet a few years ago during the O. J. Simpson trial. Since then women's groups, the press, and the medical community have scrutinized such violence in an attempt to discover its cause, and thereby a solution. Practically every medical journal that comes across my desk contains some sort of primer on the subject. Like everything else that accounts for frictions between men and women, however, domestic violence has cultural and learned components superimposed on genetic predilections. It exists on the uncomfortable continuum that runs from men verbally intimidating women all the way to physical violence. Nipping physical abuse in the bud requires that, when faced with it, women see it for what it is.

I'm not going to say much about women being physically abused within the context of a marriage or relationship, except to say that no form of it should ever be tolerated. There are no grey areas when it comes to physical abuse which, once exhibited, will nearly always recur. Women who find themselves in this predicament need to be afraid and brave at once as they extricate themselves from what will otherwise almost certainly be a progressively unfortunate circumstance. It's important to view any physical abuse or coercion very seriously and not wait or temporize hoping things will improve. The longer you stall, the more difficult it will ultimately be to emancipate yourself. Even if your life is never at stake, your mental health and sense of well-being will be. At the first sign, get serious, get help, and get out.

Some women, however, would say that getting help and getting out is not that simple, even when the potential for serious harm is pretty obvious. If this is true for an issue as black and white as physical violence, how much more difficult are the judgment calls about what is tolerable in the large grey zone of men's nonviolent intimidation of women? Such judgments are infinitely problematic. When some women don't even realize they are being intimidated, how can there be a problem, let alone a solution? And, of course, where children share the tableau, everything is much more complicated.

Abusiveness usually follows an insidious course. Once the courtship and best behavior are things of the past, married individuals often fall into patterns with which they were programmed as children. We know that physically violent partners have usually witnessed similar violence between adults in their childhoods. Patterns of nonviolent intimidation have the same origins but are much trickier to discern because, rather than being obvious outbursts, they are abstrusely sprawled all over the emotional landscape of a marriage.

I overheard a conversation recently while I was waiting to use the telephone in the ladies lounge of a large department store. A woman in her early thirties was talking rather loudly to her husband, who I gathered was at the other end of the phone watching a sporting event with several of his buddies. The woman was on her break from work and was calling to ask whether it would be all right for her to purchase an ironing board. The tone at the woman's end of the conversation was extremely solicitous: "Yes, honey, I'll be able to iron all your shirts," and "No, sweetie, I promise I won't spend a penny more." Before she bid him a carefully appreciative good-bye, she said, "Oh, and one more thing I forgot to tell you. I wrote a check for the gas bill. I hope that's okay. It is due tomorrow, so I thought you would want me to do that. That's all right? Okay. Good. I'm glad you're not mad. I'll see you after work, honey. I miss you."

I tried to be discreet and not stare as this conversation transpired. Here she was, earning her own money and not only having to ask permission for every cent she spent, but having to be obsequiously grateful when permission was granted. I was torn between grabbing this woman's arm and saying, "Are you nuts?" and leaving her to her own peculiar brand of codependence. Relationships like this describe just one point on the vast intimidation spectrum; we just don't usually witness their perversity spelled out quite so publicly.

It doesn't help that oftentimes we can't be sure what is public and what is private. The various arms of the media regularly expose the deplorable behavior of public officials who have every incentive to behave themselves. It should come as no surprise, then, that in the lower-profile spheres most of us inhabit, such behavior is epidemic. The ubiquitous disconnect between people's public and private lives fosters a false sense of tranquillity until we are jolted out of our reverie by a personal or observed event.

Recently while at a friend's home, I heard a male neighbor ranting and cursing loudly and looked at my friend for an explanation. "I don't know what goes on up there," she said, nodding her head in the direction of the house up the hill. "The police have been out once that I know of, but the wife seems like a pretty savvy player, no pushover. I have to assume she knows what she's doing. They have a little girl, and I can't imagine the wife would stick around if she thought there was any potential for violence. I think he just has a little too much to drink from time to time and gets verbally belligerent. Of course, whenever I talk to him, he's the picture of gentility."

Some women would witness a scene like this and declare with certainty that they'd never put up with it. Some of those same women, however, live daily with variations on the same marital dynamic. They just see it differently; it has permeated their own lives for so long—usually since they were children—that they don't see their own situation as aberrant, or they have found a way to justify their tolerance. Women tell themselves that family unity is more important than their own dignity or that living with marital strife is better for kids than living with a divorce. Some women opt for dependence and material comfort over independence and self-respect. The problem is that, as is the case with physical abuse, the situation won't go away or get better on its own; it almost always becomes worse.

As with physical abuse, it is up to women to see intimidation for what it is. The vicious and sometimes subtle cycle of intimidation begins the first time a girl is told not to speak to her father in a certain tone of voice or not to talk back. And although most girls are told the same thing in regard to their mothers, they quickly learn that the consequences of sassing their mother, or for that matter just letting her know how they feel about something, are rarely as uncomfortable as when they do this to Dad. Boys are told the same thing as their sisters but are often let off the hook. Girls are delivered a double whammy when they witness their mothers being intimidated by their fathers.

In addition to this, parents often do a dance of denial when children are around. Dad is irritable, unpleasant, or has had too much to drink and Mom excuses his behavior. "He's under a lot of pressure at work," she tells the kids, or she finds ways to validate Dad's feelings of entitlement when things don't go the way he would like. Mothers often do this to spare their children the emotional discomfort of a scene, but what they are doing more often is ensuring that these children will not only witness more of the same, but carry a similar dynamic into their own adult lives.

In what ways can this predicament be addressed? Making every attempt to scrutinize a mate before he becomes one is the first step, although very often the behavior isn't apparent during a courtship. This makes it all the more important that a woman recognizes her feelings of emotional discomfort when they arise, that instead of merely getting angry or resentful or submissive and moving on to the next encounter, she understands that she is being intimidated. Having identified what's going on, she needs to take it on faith that, in the absence of some sort of confrontation or intervention, she can expect more of the same.

Because we live in an imperfect world with imperfect interpersonal relationships, perfection is not the goal. Even the best marriages weather their share of conflict, disagreement, and heartache. A woman would experience these even if she lived alone. Still, when she lives with a male partner, dignity, courtesy, and mutual respect—the basics of interpersonal dealings that we all learn in kindergarten—need to provide the framework for any interaction. If a marriage partner hasn't learned these fundamentals by the time he takes his vows, it's not likely he's going to learn them any time soon or be able to model them for children. About this a woman should be very clear.

Woman, Name Thyself

The original version of feminism wasn't big on relationships. It saw an imbalance of power in marriage and an inequity of pay and power in the workplace. And in the relationships between mothers and children, it . . . well, it took a pass. It did, however, leave an invaluable legacy of possibility for subsequent versions of feminism. (Some call this postfeminism, a term I've never liked because of the implication that feminism is somehow left behind or forgotten, a dangerous notion at best.) One of the more luscious prospects of the feminist legacy was that women did not have to be swallowed whole by marriage, but could be many things to many people and still maintain their identity. The hallmark of this delightful development was the cultural, albeit gradual, acceptance of couples in which the man and woman had different last names.

This cultural acceptance shouldn't be confused with widespread approval. That Hillary Rodham had to become Hillary Rodham Clinton to appease the snippety masses was a reality check on where the majority was stuck, as recently as the early 1990s, on the subject of letting the missus be the Ms. Those of us who declined to acquire married names did so for a variety of reasons sufficient to overcome a still-persistent bias in favor of not bucking the system.

Some women decided against changing their names because, on

becoming brides of men who had already bestowed their last name on a prior wife, they were less than enthusiastic about becoming Mrs. So-and-So number two, opting instead to remain Themself number one. Others were saving a surname on the brink of extinction. Still others were making a preemptive statement about dependency. But many women just didn't see the sense in forfeiting a name that had served them well for what had up until then been a lifetime.

Push came to shove for me when I filled out the application for a marriage license. I had to decide who I was going to be for the rest of my life: my father's daughter or my husband's wife. As it happened, I had never thought of my name as being anyone's but mine, and it had served me well through college and most of medical school. I guess I also knew too many women who were stringing last names together like beads on a choker as they progressed to sequential husbands. I kept my name; that way, no matter what happened, at least I'd know who I was.

Regardless of the reason for doing so, keeping your name is a walk in the park until Baby Boy or Baby Girl So-and-So shows up. Suddenly there is all this explaining to do, not to mention yet another identity crisis: am I me or am I this child's mother? The intensity with which women come into motherhood often loosens prior boundaries, and hyphens begin to show up in names where there were none before. Like an addendum to the original marriage agreement (which children, whether planned or not, certainly are), many women tack their husband's name on to their own with a hyphen. Another way around the dilemma is to hyphenate the child's name, which doubles the jeopardy down the line when that child takes a spouse. Some women keep their—now maiden—names for professional purposes and adopt the "family" (read "husband's") name for personal use. Men meanwhile, at least those who don't adopt aliases, enter and leave this world with one and the same surname.

One couple I know adopted a European version of family-name assignment. The woman in this case was the very last of her family who could possibly carry on the family name. Before marriage (way to go!) she made a pact with her husband-to-be. Their first boy would get her last name; any other children would be given his. They went on to produce one girl (his last name) and one boy (her last name). As she relates the effect of this ten years into the arrangement, she finds bonuses she could never have envisioned. "When there is a dispute," she muses with a smile, "we can line up evenly in all sorts of ways—last name against last name, boys against girls, or kids against parents. It's all terribly fair."

Aside from the fact that even sophisticated software will have a time of it keeping track of all this ad-libbed lineage, you wonder what Generation Hyphen will do. The up-and-coming marital deals might include, "You drop one name and I'll drop one name and we'll hyphenate what's left," or, "Let's put all our different names in an empty baby-wipes box and have a drawing. The winning name will serve us and our posterity—at least until they get married."

This system will work for the amiable among us, but the name game can also be a true test of machismo. An acquaintance of mine who had staunchly maintained her surname (her hurname?) did the flip-flop number when her first child arrived. In this case, it wasn't her preference to unite under one banner, but her husband's. She found herself hedging to accommodate him, and after a while she wasn't sure how to introduce herself and when. In her office she was Dr.; to her kid's teachers she was Mrs.; and to her friends she was the safest of all, her first name only. One day, twelve years and three kids into her marriage, she mentioned to me that the whole sordid subject was still driving her crazy. "I have this recurrent dream," she confided. "I'm asleep and the phone rings, and when I answer it this telemarketer wants to know what last name she should put on my credit cards. My husband is listening, and I don't know what to tell her. Pretty soon I'm so conflicted and miserable that I wake up sweating."

I too had a brief run-in with my husband's feelings on this subject. Despite his mother making a point to tell me before I married her son that when she changed her name to her husband's it was the happiest moment of her life, my husband genuinely supported my decision not to become his Mrs. When my oldest daughter was ten, however, she challenged not his male pride, but his fatherly pride, by deciding to use my last name. Everyone at her school fell into line with her wishes and before long every paper, art project, tuition bill, and textbook was inscribed with her first name and my last. I was amused and curious about her change of heart but chalked it up to identity development and let things happen. My husband, however, had a hard time with it.

Two years later I finally learned the reason for my daughter's change of heart. Her initials had sounded too much like an elementary school slang word for a female body part (not even spelled correctly), and she had been teased. Of course, she never told us this at the time. Midway through her first year of junior high school, when she needed to produce her birth certificate for a swimming competition, she decided—elementary school rhymes being a thing of the past—that she'd just switch back. This made for an interesting conversation between me and her counselor at school when I called to say that the name the school had on their records wasn't my daughter's real name. In no time, her identity had changed again and everyone, especially my husband, was happy.

But even a determined original name sayer like myself flinches from time to time. Until they started junior high and high school, my kids and I lived on a first-name basis with just about everyone in their lives including friends, teachers, and other parents. As their lives and schedules mushroomed, all of a sudden there were people besides the Little League coach who wanted to make me a Mrs. Teachers, coaches, other parents, and all of my children's teenaged friends addressed me as Mrs. My-Kids'-Last-Name. It's probably best that it took so long for this to happen because by then I had softened—not capitulated, mind you, but softened. I no longer felt annoyed at the presumption, nor did I correct everyone who presumed. The threat of being anyone but myself had come and gone, and with it the threat of somehow being less than my kids' mother because we had different last names. A mother by any other name, I've found, is still the mom.

Don't Worry, Be Healthy

The very best preparation for whatever life path you choose is, of course, to be in physical and emotional shape to pursue it. During the late teens and twenties, good health is mostly taken for granted, yet the habits developed during these years influence what comes next. But even for those who take an active interest in their health, the dos and don'ts are not always easy to decipher, whether in early, mid, or late adulthood.

"New clinical studies show there are no answers," attests one of those little lapel buttons. Were it not so discouragingly close to the truth, this might actually be funny. We are all—doctors and patients alike—continually barraged with contradictory evidence regarding the best way to enhance our health and avoid illness. Somewhere in what emerges from the gobbledy-gook of money-making schemes, warring experts, and various studies-of-the-moment, we are supposed to be able to discern the truth about how to best care for ourselves. Who could blame a person for throwing up her hands in despair when the laundry list of what to watch out for runs the gamut from social drinking to sun and from black hair dye to barbecued beef.

It's overwhelming to think that you have to exercise daily; keep fat consumption to no more than 20 percent of your daily calories; avoid alcohol, caffeine, and cigarettes; take calcium and antioxidant vitamins; have your first child before age thirty; eat lots of broccoli; have safe sex; and minimize stress in order to dodge the cancer bullet and keep your heart healthy. The problem, of course, is that—even if a person were willing and able to do all this—the recommendations for many of these variables change so regularly that one week we hear that even low-level activities like gardening and vacuuming qualify as adequate adult physical education, while the next week's wisdom is that it takes four hours of fairly rigorous exercise to do the trick. When it comes to advice about exercise, estrogen replacement, fat intake, caffeine consumption, and vitamin supplementation, opinions seem to differ from one physician to the next, one magazine to the next, and one minute to the next. So what's a woman to do?

As with most things, there is a reasonable approach to optimal health for those who are able to let the fads come and go without getting way-laid by them. Enough reliable information has risen to the surface of the morass of medical sound bites over the past ten years to provide a rational guide to personal health. To keep from getting stuck in minutiae every time a new health concept is introduced on the six o'clock news, it's smart to focus on the big picture and pursue a determined yet moderate approach to self-health care. Here is my take on the eight most important health concepts that have emerged over the past decade. Sorry, I can't offer a magic bullet, a single pill, a sexy-sounding scenario, or an eat-every-thing-in-sight diet. I can predict, though, that if you attempt this fairly simple approach to everyday life—the same one you've heard from all sources of common sense but will never read on the cover of tabloids or slick magazines—you will feel your best.

One: Don't smoke. I hate to begin with a prohibition, but number one on my health-enhancement list is don't smoke. The addictive nature of it notwithstanding, this one is really simple. It involves no calorie counting, no percentage figuring, takes no time, and will save money. Most importantly, this one thing alone will prolong your life, make you smell better, and give you a leg up on the next item on the list.

Two: Exercise. Before I begin the sermon, know this: The morning I opened the newspaper to headlines proclaiming "Just Four Hours of Exercise Each Week Dramatically Lowers Women's Risk of Breast Cancer," I was profoundly discouraged. Despite my dedication to regular exercise, I am rarely able to squeeze out four full hours in a week. Every time I try to pound the stair stepper before getting the kids to school, the entire morning goes into the toilet and everyone is at each other's throats by the time we get into the car. If I wait until after school starts, it cuts terminally into my work time. After school and evenings aren't even possible; then I get up and repeat everything again the following day. Still I keep chasing an exercise dream and somehow work out enough to feel marginally virtuous about it from time to time. So I don't appreciate it when researchers start setting up impossible guidelines. How about three hours, fellas? That's thirty minutes, six days a week with a rest on the seventh day. It'll have to do for most weeks.

My sob story notwithstanding, I'm going to tell you to exercise regularly and briskly for thirty to sixty minutes at a time as many times each week as you can possibly manage it. If you at least aspire to this goal, you'll be headed in the right direction. What exactly these parameters mean will differ from one person to the next depending on a number of factors like age, weight, background, and tendency toward inertia. If you have it in you and your schedule to run five miles each day, go for it. If not, perhaps you have a baby in a stroller or a dog, or both, and are motivated to walk for forty-five minutes daily. Or maybe you're like me and combine reading and exercise by climbing up onto a stair stepper for your daily huffing and puffing. You need to figure out what will work best for your individual situation and keep it up for at least thirty minutes at a time.

The most important feature of the method you choose is not so much that it set sweat records as that it be enjoyable. When I took up soccer at the unlikely age of forty, I did so to learn the game and to be able to competently coach my kids. The benefit, despite a number of inevitable injuries, was far greater than my initial expectation. I found that no matter how fed up I was with my husband, no matter how emotionally pummeled I was feeling from the relentlessness of tending to several small children, and regardless of what sorts of frustrations I was experiencing in my work, just running after a ball and kicking it hard for ninety minutes a couple of times a week made everything seem much better. If you view exercise as one more thing to worry about or as an unpleasant necessity, you'll never get enough of it. But when you do something—be it tennis, golf, group aerobics, ice skating, swimming, or even gardening—even if it's something different each day, you'll be strengthening bone, protecting your heart, making your body more reliable, and generating a sense of well-being that will accompany you for the rest of the day. Active living, day in and day out, is the key to exercise success.

Three: Diet for Good Nutrition. Predictably, the next thing on my list is nutrition, or diet. Not diet as in the Ice Cream Sundae Diet or the Grapefruit and Prune Juice Diet or the Designer Nutritional Product Diet, but diet as in the everything-you-eat-each-day diet. Our national thin wish is so compelling that something as basic to survival as eating is the target of one gimmick after another. That women fall for these schemes more often than men puts us at risk of seeming less intelligent. So for the sake of your sisters if not your own health, forget the fad diets and get a life—a sound nutritional life.

Diets fall into three categories: the eat-it category, which constitutes the foundation for the now well-known advice to consume five to six helpings of fruits and vegetables a day; the don't-eat-it category, which motivates the current fat phobia; and the calories-in-equal-calories-out category, which is the basis of most dietary denial. Here's what you need to know.

Eat-it nutrition. In the eat-it category, science has now demonstrated what parents have been telling kids for years: eating fruits and vegetables is good for you. It is so good, in fact, that plain old fruits and vegetables comprise the most potent anticancer agents available to us. These foods contain phytochemicals that, at least in their natural form, protect against a variety of cancers. Of course, eating fruits and vegetables isn't as convenient as taking a pill, gobbling a snack bar, or supplementally powdering a shake.

Yet convenience, as anyone who has ever owned an electric can opener can attest, is not always what it's cracked up to be. None of the supplements have been proven to be as effective as the real thing. Perhaps because something in a turnip besides the phytochemical is necessary for the protective effect, or because the extraction process inactivates some aspect of the phytochemical, or because broccoli by any other name is not as potent (for some yet to be determined reason), nothing has been found to be as good for you as eating a wide variety of fruits and veggies every day.

Don't-eat-it diets. Fats and sugars are in the don't-eat-it category. These nutritional public enemies have gotten a worse rap than they deserve because of the tendency to confuse bestsellers with sound advice. It is true that as a group, Americans eat too much fat, but then as a group we eat too much of everything. We also hang on to vague notions about what we should eat far after such practices have been shown to be misguided. I still see mothers nodding their heads in approval while their child gobbles a fast-food burger because, after all, the kid is getting her protein (never mind the sauce dripping down the kid's fingers or the requisite french fries). And I still hear parents blame behavioral meltdowns on sugar rather than on the party itself. We act more like flies around flypaper when it comes to dietary notions than like the educable adults we surely are.

My philosophy about fat is pretty simple. Although I am an unabashed admirer of Dr. Dean Ornish and the work he has done with severely ill cardiac patients, I like to think that if good habits are put in place at an early age, the next generation won't have to heel to a diet that takes only 10 percent of its calories from fat. For individuals who don't have a genetic predisposition to cardiac disease, I recommend a daily food intake that allots calories as follows: 20 to 30 percent from fat (I don't distinguish between saturated and unsaturated fat but look to the quality of the fat; avocados or nuts, for instance, are certainly preferable to a stick of margarine), 25 to 35 percent from protein (it takes less than you think to get this much), and about 45 to 55 percent from carbohydrates (as in fruits, vegetables, and whole grains).

Calories in equals calories out for a happy weight. The whole topic of nutrition and exercise often sends people—women in particular—into weird psychological zones. Our national obsession with female stick figures has emotionally etched many a girl, teen, and mature woman with chronic lines of unhappiness and self-loathing. Women chase an impossible ideal created by the fashion industry despite the fact that thin does not necessarily mean fit and vice versa. One of the most helpful things a woman can do for herself is to find a happy weight and nurture it. The operative word here is *happy*, which by definition does not include self-torture in its pursuit. In the lingo of the now obsolete weight-reduction (read fen-phen) clinics, this weight is called a "set point," and, yes, sometimes it is elusive and can use some calorie-counting encouragement or, in extreme cases, medical help. But the woman who is forever trying to starve or medicate away that extra ten or fifteen pounds hasn't come to terms with her happy weight, nor does she understand that the set point settles where calories consumed equal calories burned. This concept—not all-or-nothing, no-fat, carbohydrate-counting, wheat grass, or liquid diets—is the key to maintaining a happy weight.

Four: Be sun smart. So now you're smokeless, you've exercised well, you're munching on an apple, and you think you've earned a little downtime on the chaise lounge in the backyard (on the roof?). All right, take 45—45 SPF, that is—and be sun smart.

Whether because the ozone layer is truly dispersing, or because we've become expert at spending time outdoors, or because we're living longer, the sun is doing a number on our skin. While the skin cancer beast—symbolic of the rising incidence of skin cancer—is growing all the time, there are ways to tame it. You can stay out of the sun or under an umbrella, a tactic which, though complete, has its limitations; you can wear a hat while outdoors, although the most popular type, the baseball cap, doesn't protect the ears which are the most common site of skin cancer; and you can be conscientious and thorough about using sunscreen. Doing some or all of these is your best bet for avoiding sun worshiper's remorse as you add candles to your cakes.

Five: Practice safe sex. For the sake of alliteration and not because sun and sex are cosmically related, I move to the recommendation that it is important to practice safe sex. This one should be a no-brainer, but since brains rarely enter into decisions about sex I'll say it anyway. Regard the guy who tells you that condoms interfere with his ability to perform sexually as a throwback and do just that with him. There are—have faith in this—plenty of other fish in the sea who will care more about you than about putting you at risk for the sake of their machismo.

Six: Ask for help when you need it. Of course, once you've thrown back that guy or had an argument with your husband; been given too much work by your boss; or gotten bad news from your mechanic, computer consultant, or doctor—you may feel depressed. Sooner or later, just about everyone has a bout with the blues and needs to be able to ask for help. Great strides have been made over the past decade in identifying and medically treating depression. Although medication isn't always the answer, it can be extremely helpful, especially for those whose depression is of a long-term, chronic nature. Despite the information that the brain has given up about its chemical comings and goings, and despite the dazzling responses some folks have shown in response to antidepressants, there remain those for whom talk therapy—sometimes in combination with medication—is a necessary part of any recovery process. It does no good, for instance, for a woman who is depressed because of an abusive spouse or a pattern of making bad choices in men to have an antidepressant be her only therapeutic modality. She needs the insight and the help to make changes that talk therapy provides in order to move through and beyond her depression.

Seven: Nurture a few good friendships. The foregoing notwithstanding, very often the best talk therapy isn't found in a therapist's office but in a conversation with a good friend. The mind-and-body folks are showing convincingly, albeit not surprisingly, that a good support group—a network as we say—can be as good as any medicine when it comes to healing the body or the mind. Nurture a few good friendships and the inevitable downtimes won't seem so low, nor last so long. And while you're at it, get good at divesting yourself of or avoiding toxic friendships, the ones that take much more than they give or that seem to feed the very anger, frustration, sadness, or confusion you're trying to work out.

Eight: Get medicine when appropriate. Finally, number eight on the self-care schedule is an odd recommendation: Avail yourself of what medicine has to offer when you need it. I call this better living through chemistry and include it here because of the self-defeating skepticism (as opposed to a healthy skepticism) and mistrust of conventional medicine that seems to afflict so many women. To be sure, research establishments and medical authorities have invited some of this wariness in a number of ways: by virtue of not recognizing women's special research needs until relatively recently, by abiding numerous conflicting expert positions, and by just plain not being able to say, "We don't know," from time to time. However and unfortunately, because the physician-is-God mentality is tenacious, sometimes a woman doesn't want to be told that there is no magic bullet for her particular dilemma.

A few of the things that represent real medical progress but are still held in suspicion by many include routine well-woman screening with a pap smear, routine (I suggest annual) mammograms after age forty, post-menopausal hormone-replacement therapy (in the absence of specific risk factors), and the aforementioned antidepressant medications. These are life-prolonging items that, because they are not "natural," whatever that means, are often underutilized. Be careful of that word, *natural*, when invoked in support of your health; nature offers up some powerful healing agents in conjunction with some potent toxic ones. One of the very worst drug reactions I ever came across, for instance, resulted from the "natural" Chinese herb *ma huang*. The purpose of conventional medicine is to harness nature's capacity to heal and make it widely available.

There you have it. A distillation of the most important ways to care for your health. Even what may seem like the most obvious of these recommendations have had to earn respectability by being examined and reexamined by researchers. The problem with medical progress is that it relies on studies to verify or disprove various theories. Each study is subject to numerous glitches, errors in analysis, confounding factors, and design problems, so that a single study, regardless of how long it takes to execute, is not something on which to hang a hat. Very often it takes years and many studies to make a credible case for an idea, a procedure, or even a life-saving drug. In the meantime, it's possible to go crazy trying to hang on to every suggestion that makes its way out of the medical research community via the media. Don't get discouraged or sidelined by the demands of trends but rather, honor the basics for better health.

Chapter Two

Women Still Have the Babies

Why was it that so many women artists who had renounced having children could then paint nothing but mothers and children?

—Erica Jong

Making the switch from being single, independent, and self-directed to being married and contemplating motherhood is, in itself, an existential sea change, yet one eventually dwarfed by the actual act of becoming a mother. The alterations in a woman's self-image, sense of purpose, relationships, emotional complexion, and hormonal equilibrium that occur in the aftermath of labor and delivery defy thorough preparation; the magnitude of the push and pull is rarely anticipated. Still, a sound combination of education, intuition, and insight will serve a new mom well, enabling her to heed and learn from the inevitable reality checks that will come her way during these very complex adjustments.

Take Your Life in Your Own Hands

Doing the same thing over and over again for eons has a way of creating assumptions. Since before recorded history women have grown up, partnered with men, borne and raised children, and died. The time elapsed since the introduction of effective birth control a half century ago is but a fraction of a second on the time line of *Homo sapiens*. Yet the interval has been anthropologically momentous. Having control over reproduction has meant that women are no longer mandated to follow biological manifest destinies. From a technological standpoint, women can choose not only when, but whether to have children.

The scientific progress that led to the development of birth control led at the same time to other medical developments. Women, who at the beginning of the twentieth century lived to be only about forty or fifty, now live nearly twice that long. For those a century ago who lived long enough to experience it, menopause was not the beginning of a whole new phase of life as it is now, but part of a permanent denouement. That there is now life after menopause has resulted in some interesting postponements of gratification—such as women in their sixties deciding to have babies. But more important, such life expectancies have opened up a huge range of possibilities to all postmenarchical women.

Our biological brains, however, have not kept pace with technology. From an intellectual standpoint we get it. We can put off having children until after we're done with college or grad school or even until we've made a name for ourselves in our chosen field. We can discuss with our partners how many kids we want and when. We can even decide we don't want to have children at all. Sooner or later, however, most women come upon their evolutionarily established desire to become mothers, and rational planning takes a backseat to the brain chemistry that shapes obsession. And while this is distinctly in the best interests of our species, it is not always in the individual best interests of a modern working woman. Scientific feminism tamed the reproductive cycle's biology, but how to nip this cycle in its emotional bud remains enigmatic. As a result, our best intellectually guided birth-control intentions are frequently derailed by other—often more compelling—eons-old instincts.

This heart-head dilemma is compounded by the human tendency to gravitate toward romantic involvements. Even terribly sensible women get sidetracked by romance and cease to think clearly at crucial moments. If birth control is in place at these times, it works; if not, other well-known consequences may ensue. Even in its ideal form, however, reproductive choice creates ambivalence. Most women, sooner or later and whether heterosexual or not, want to have a baby. This desire can be triggered by a host of things: a bad relationship (a baby will fix it, right?); a good relationship; progressing age (although when a twenty-five-year-old cites this, the irrationality of the phenomenon becomes apparent); loneliness; the need to do something higher and harder than whatever has already been achieved (a notch on Superwoman's belt); or, of course, a genuine, well-thought-out desire to have children.

In responding to any of these, the long-term ramifications of motherhood are rarely considered, partly because heat-of-the-moment decisions are not made with the future in mind and partly because as a culture we are not very good at teaching about what comes next for adult women faced with childbearing and child-rearing decisions. We are pretty good at teaching about reproductive biology, safe sex, abusive relationships, the evils of drugs and alcohol, and the trappings of perfunctory moralism. In other words we don't shy away from teaching about premarital sexual issues, a necessary if not always effective undertaking. Nonetheless, a girl rarely hears the truth about what happens *after* the marriage, *after* the baby, *after* the too-good-to-be-true job offer. Our collective mantra tends to be "You can have it all," and depression and unhappiness be damned.

A friend summed this up well one day when, emotionally wide-eyed about having begun a new job while simultaneously trying to stay maximally invested in her two young sons, she was fumbling for her next step. She had been hired to assist a professor in writing a book and was thrilled to have the intellectual stimulation of the project and the university setting after having stayed at home with her then eight- and three-year-old boys since the oldest was born. Every day, however, seemed to throw another unexpected wrench into the works. Her younger son had a series of ear infections that made the preschool arrangement only intermittently reliable for child-care purposes. Then, as soon as one child was well, the other became homebound with a series of allergy-related symptoms. This woman had a very understanding, helpful husband whose work schedule was almost infinitely flexible. Nonetheless, after giving it their best effort for six months, they both admitted to being at their wits' end. She resigned her position, and he resumed the task of being sole breadwinner. "Nobody ever told me," my friend said, shaking her head about the whole thing one day, "that choices would have to be made and prices paid."

One of the most important concepts young women of childbearing age should know well—at least as reflexively as they know the price of cosmetics, the latest fashion imperatives, their maximal heart rate, or the particulars of a business meeting—is that having a baby will affect their lives immutably. And while there may be no perfect time to become a mom, once done, the practical aspects of life may become uncomfortable for those who believe that a baby is but a blip on the radar screen of ambition. The logistics of everything a woman wants to do thereafter, be it work or leisure-related, will be more difficult. Passions and priorities will rearrange themselves naturally; a work schedule will not.

Because child rearing takes a toll, it is not for every woman. It has its unmistakable rewards, but also its nonnegotiable price. And although the ability to say yes or no to motherhood is one of the luxuries of the birth-control era, motherhood is still culturally viewed not as a luxury but as a command performance. I say culturally here because even women who have major reservations about their suitability for the job of raising kids are made to feel that they will be missing out on a defining experience should they decide to forego it. The problem with this societal presumption is that there are many ways to define being a mother, some better and some more abysmal than others, so that just being identified as a mum doesn't assume a happy circumstance.

More and more women are exercising their options in this regard and choosing to be single or married without children. Are they missing out? The answer to this lies in how they decide to otherwise fill their lives because, make no mistake, children, especially more than one, will fill an enormous section of a woman's life. So, however, will uncountable other pursuits or passions, and therein lies the choice.

Pace Yourself

The panoply of choices available to women at the millennium invites overambitiousness rather than careful choosing. Even as I regard my teenaged daughter biting off huge chunks of experience at once, I want to say, "Easy does it. Take one or two things at a time. You don't have to do everything just because it's there." She in turn views me and my notions—that a leisurely meal, day off, or walk on the beach would do her good—the way I viewed my college calculus course, as an annoying obstacle on my fast track to where I was going. Is this the example my generation has set for her, the example I've set?

For many young women, life is an irresistible smorgasbord of possibilities. To start with an appetizer and work your way systematically through the salad course, entrée, and dessert takes too much patience, self-control, or time. For the young and ambitious, the sequence of things is secondary to the opportune time, which is now. Alas, you have to agree; life is not as simple as ordering dinner in a restaurant, and next times can be elusive. Still, this doesn't mean there isn't a logical progression to life's feast or that whatever reaches the table won't affect what is ordered next. It may not be possible to get precisely what you want, but it's also not advisable to eat all the desserts first.

The fact that women have the intellectual capacity of rocket scientists, the biological capabilities of mothers, the learned and inherent talents of nurturers, and the socially imposed responsibilities of domestic managers does not mean that all these pieces will fit neatly together at once. It only indicates what should be obvious after thirty years of a trial-and-error approach to reckoning all these concomitant features: you may be able to have it all eventually, but you can't do it all simultaneously. And while the practical implications of this are not complicated, it can take a while to sort it all out.

When I set my sights on being a physician, the traditional approach to this ambition was spelled out quite clearly. You completed a premed major in college with exemplary grades, did well on the MCAT exams, had something extracurricular to say about yourself on the med school applications, then with any luck or knowledge of the right people, spent four years in medical school and several years as a resident. Having paid these dues, you could enter private or group practice, do research, administrate, or teach. It all fell into place along a nice straight line.

The logical way for a woman to proceed, however, was not nearly as obvious. Nor, for that matter, was there even a notion that a woman might tackle this rather imposing endeavor differently than a man. The Zeitgeist of the 1970s still turned on an axis of great expectations begotten of paltry experience. Women were doing the smorgasbord thing and I thought the desserts (motherhood) looked pretty good, so I started on those partway through the appetizer of medical school. The main course—residency and medical practice—were shortchanged as a result. Not many people, after all, finish their entrée right after dessert.

I set out to doctordom on the traditional path because I subscribed to the prevailing notion that women had been held down in suboptimally productive roles and less than meaningful lives as homemakers. I saw these productivity and meaning gaps as yawning chasms, waiting to be filled by a career and not just any career. It had to be the all-encompassing kind like fathers had. No one ever said that the chasms weren't quite as gaping as they were made out to be or that it wouldn't require a career in medicine to fill the gap between what my mother did with her time and my father with his. The more disdainful feminists portrayed children and domestic responsibilities as a sideline, a diversion, a mere hobby. Anyone who saw motherhood as anywhere near a full-time occupation, went the thinking, was a ninny.

To make matters worse, men were still asking why they should expend valuable resources training women for jobs that these same women would abandon at the first twinge of labor. This attitude was dangled in front of my fellow college women like a taunt. We went for the jugular of this theory by pursuing the highest, hardest, fastest career tracks we could. And we did it the way the guys told us to. There was just one glitch, a major one. Before many of us could say, "So there!" we were waylaid by our biological clocks.

This was at a time when, even if you only read a small-town local newspaper, there was an underlying current of propagation panic in what was being written about "liberated" career women. If you didn't have babies when you were young, went the sure-to-sell media wisdom, chances were you'd never be able to have them. Fertility was made out to be so precarious an attribute that you wondered how our species had managed to survive and propagate. The fact that enormous numbers of women in their late thirties and early forties were having healthy babies was ignored by the fertility-panic mongers.

Then there were the statistics about breast cancer: women who had their first child before age thirty were at lower risk than those who waited. And of course, there were other things we hadn't counted on—like the fact that male bosses and colleagues were often going home to wives and children, while we female career manics were staying after hours to prove ourselves and spending lonely weekends alone or muddling through stress-ridden temporary relationships. That the cumulative effect of all this didn't see women en masse putting their careers on the back burner in deference to marriage and motherhood speaks to a faith in the new social order with which my female peers had come of age.

The timing differed for everyone, of course. Some insightful women managed to put a lock on their professional reputations before mixing in motherhood. Another fortunate few married liberated guys who were as good as their word about doing the dirty work required to combine family and career. Some women dropped out completely and became brilliant homemakers with volunteer résumés pages long. But many others of us who chose to have children did it less decisively, stopping work here for a few weeks or months and starting there, cutting back here and gearing up again there, taking a family leave here and making up for it there—all in an effort to keep our hands in the sacred "it." Consequently, we drove ourselves, if not our bosses and partners, crazy. Careers were supposed to cut straight lines through our lives, not jog all over the map. But all anyone really knew about careers was framed conspicuously in the male experience. Only a small minority of women had ever tried juxtaposing motherhood with demanding careers.

We called it juggling because that's what it was, not cleverly artful entertainment, but a precarious undertaking. We were not juggling oranges or even lit torches, but the essentials of our existence. Yet at any moment you might miss a catch, and the whole delicately balanced arrangement would tumble, revealing your vulnerable reality. You'd call in sick because the kid was sick one day, then you'd be so preoccupied by a meeting the next day that you'd forget preschool lasted only a half day and would have to make a mad dash in response to a phone call from the school's director. The fact that even in the best of circumstances plans were never more than tentative was bad enough. That we were in denial about it made it much worse; you can't fix what you can't or won't see.

Nonetheless, young mothers making difficult choices often don't think in entirely logical terms. They are in the thick of it, doing what has to be done while following rudimentary instincts. They follow contradictory signposts erected by their predecessors along previously mapped but seriously potholed roads to career development and motherhood. Even with the benefit of hindsight, I know it would have been foolish of me to abandon medicine, particularly at the junction of medical school and internship, simply for fear of leaving my baby with a sitter. Like every other parent, working or not, I made compromises, but none that impeded my heart's ability to hear my children over the noise of my career. Still, the conflicts I encountered would almost certainly have been more amenable to resolution had I waited until after medical school to have my first child. I never considered this option, however, because the only road signs I saw said "Do it all. Go for it now. Supermomdom awaits."

Yet the no-man's-land (literally) of straddling two worlds was not impossible, nor even necessarily unpleasant. The way it went for any individual depended substantially on the availability of backup resources, both human and financial. Still, when it went badly, the brunt of the unhappiness, stress, or financial displacement was invariably visited disproportionately on the woman. Those who had taken a stepwise approach to their adult lives and completed and become good at their breadwinning roles before having children were at a distinct advantage when it came to structuring their futures. Not only could they bargain from a position of strength when the subject of maternity leave or family time came up, but they weren't trapped in funky marriages solely because of financial dependence.

Putting a career only partially in place before stepping out even briefly to start a family makes it more difficult to step back in at the same level of performance and income. Confidence plays a part in your ability to maneuver through unpredictable territory. Getting good at how you make money and becoming valuable to and admired by your boss or colleagues makes any bargaining—whether with yourself, your husband, or your employer—more likely to go in your favor. Competence also supplies a versatility to those who decide to work at home or part-time or both.

Just as there is no perfect time to get married, buy a home, or pursue a dream, there is no perfect time to have a baby. The whole endeavor is not terribly compatible with control freaks. There are, nonetheless, intervals during which a baby will change your life more or less, for better or worse. And while I don't suggest waiting until age forty to begin a large family, these intervals bear consideration. Interrupting professional school, sidelining postgraduate training, or suspending practical experience in your profession for a baby will only steepen the slope of your hill to happiness. Waiting a year, even several, may make all the difference. Not just for your future, but for your child's as well.

As I'm always tempted to tell my daughter: Life is like a meal. Slow down; stay a while; do lunch.

Kiss the Status Quo Good-Bye

A hundred years from now, when science has genetically engineered things so that all sheep are identical and breast cancer is a thing of the past, men may be getting pregnant and experiencing labor and delivery. Until then, however, some biological and psychological realities attend parenthood. Particularly where infants and toddlers are concerned, mothers tend to be more inclined than fathers to go the messy, sleep-deprived, life-interrupted distance in postponing gratification. This may be partly because they are better able to appreciate the immediate gratification, such as it is.

Every time I hear a woman, large of belly and advanced in months of a pregnancy, insist with gentle determination that "This baby is not going to change things," I bite my tongue. Well, yes, there will be a crib in the next room and an infant seat in the car, a baby-sitter to hire now and then, and an extra load of laundry from time to time, but nothing major. She and her husband will still be number one in each other's hearts, and life will be much the same—only with three rather than two. Like a nine-year-old predicting her own teen years with expectations of clean living, academic excellence, abstention from all vices, and total harmony with her parents, a first-time expectant mom can only rely on her experience to date in anticipating the future. But a prepartum woman differs substantially—in heart, soul, and outlook on the world—from a mum.

Once upon a time before the sixties, pregnant women made a leap of faith in dedicating themselves prospectively to the well-being of the up-and-coming infant. Of course there were few alternatives on this count, and mothers-to-be were in the extensive company of all the other moms whose destinies were mapped for them at their own births. The pre-sixties Zeitgeist held that men worked and women stayed home to nest, neaten, and nurture. This arrangement, as we now know, was rather confining for many women, but what recommended it was the time and emotional space it created for those up-and-coming infants. When motherhood in the abstract became, overnight, motherhood in the flesh, there was time to adjust to the enormous rearrangement of priorities that accompanied this transmogrification. It didn't matter that, where changes of the heart were concerned, women couldn't see it coming. No professional penalties like job loss, demotion, or disappointed employers awaited these unsuspecting new mothers. A six-week maternity leave didn't tick away like a time bomb waiting to blow peace of mind if not domestic tranquillity to bits and pieces.

Yet pregnancy, as anyone who has experienced it will attest, is not something you try on for size before deciding whether you're up to its aftermath. You need to expect the unexpected and be ready for anything.

My first inkling that I wasn't destined to be one of those blissfully full-bellied, soft-focused moms in the commercials for baby formulas came about six weeks into my first pregnancy. In the course of a day or two, the wellness center in my brain was commandeered by some nasty alien presence that made getting out of bed each morning an enormous obstacle to getting through a day in the life of a medical student. Nausea became the norm and energy a distant memory. I took hope from predictions that "morning sickness" would abate at three months, although the fact that mine was all-day sickness should have alerted me to what was in store. For the remainder of my pregnancy I dragged my misshapen, gaggy being around, eventually consigning myself to a life of misery. (My husband said that if he hadn't known I was pregnant, he'd have sworn I had some malignant cancer.) And then, miraculously, in the space of a few moments, albeit after prolonged labor, I was delivered from my malaise and handed the imagined alien commando who turned out to be neither alien nor nasty. It was a girl, I named her Vanessa, and my life has never even been remotely the same since.

Everything anyone has ever said about having a baby is true. All those quotes from mothers' journals, all the gushy texts in greeting cards, all the sitcom one-liners, all the grandmotherly wisdom and hindsight—all of it, true. There is a reason why new mothers talk about their labors and deliveries with only the slightest provocation and keep talking until everyone within earshot is politely excusing themselves from the conversation. It is an attempt to quantify a transcendental experience. It's a way of saying, "My soul—my heart—has been cracked open and all these emotional sensations are taking me in a million different directions at once. I'm not sure how to talk or walk or be me anymore because, with this new indescribably blissful, anxious, sober, vulnerable, delirious dimension to my motivations, I'm not sure I am still me."

But most new mothers don't say this for fear of being accused of postpartum wigginess. Instead, they talk about what can be described more sanely and concretely: their contractions, or what they were doing when their membranes ruptured (water doesn't break), or how needy of or repulsed by their husbands they suddenly became. In order to be judged sane, they talk rationally about an unfathomable experience.

That experience, however, both arms and disarms. The psychological fluidity and exhilaration that follows delivery allows most women to assume the exhausting task of mothering, but at the same time puts a crack in the armor of those who, at least in the abstract, think having a baby is just a rung on the ladder they've been climbing all their lives. Women who have lived by the I-can-do-anything credo hit their biggest glitch not in the face of college tuition or graduate school or bar exams, but on the single upward step from being just plain Superwoman to being Supermom. So consuming, then, is the postpartum experience that the career commitment necessary to qualify for the Super part of the Supermom label takes on new less ardent proportions vis-à-vis the Mom part. Nature conquers nurture in ways none can anticipate regardless of how many millions of women give birth or how ready you think you are when this baby arrives to change everything.

Don't Kid Yourself

No sooner has a woman taken her first postpartum breath than everyone she knows is ready with advice. The pediatrician tells her to sleep whenever the baby sleeps, and although she dutifully attempts to follow this prescription, she finds it impossible (and, she thinks, unnecessary). People who should know better—her mother, mother-in-law, friends, employer, siblings, and husband—make it sound like becoming a mother, becoming a family, is one big hurrah and amenable to prepartum logic. A 1,680-page copy of Mrs. Beeton's *Book of Household Management* (Ward, Lock & C., n.d.), given as a gift in 1934 (judging from the inscription) and which my mother found in a thrift shop in 1974, describes this phenomenon:

> The knowledge of the management of infants, like the mother's love for her offspring, seems to be born with the child, and to be a direct intelligence of Nature. It may thus, at first, appear as inconsistent and presumptuous to tell a woman how to rear her infant as to instruct her in the manner of loving it. Yet, though Nature is unquestionably the best nurse, Art makes so admirable a foster mother, that no sensible woman, in her novitiate of parent, would refuse the admonitions of art, or the teachings of experience, to consummate her duties of nurse.

Of course, Mrs. Beeton was writing at a time when the mechanics and how-tos of handling an infant—the nurse part—were the main consideration of the new mother. And these, as Mrs. B. points out, are teachable skills. Many women today find themselves in a predicament after delivering a baby that is far less amenable to instruction: the need to be many things to many people besides their newborn. It is this dichotomy between the assumptions of a pregnant woman and those of a new mother that distinguishes prepartum logic, with its linear supposition that one thing follows reasonably from another, from postpartum logic's lack of predictability.

The day I came home from the hospital with my first child, she slept for five hours. What's the big deal, I thought. This is a piece of cake. I even made dinner, lit candles, and clinked glasses with my husband to celebrate our cleverness in creating a baby, surviving a miserable pregnancy, and still being able to sit down to dinner together in such a civilized manner. As I raised the first bite of food to my mouth, a strange—new to our house anyway—sound filtered down the hall from the nursery. From that day to this, I have never taken the great pleasure of an uninterrupted meal for granted. I learned quickly to appreciate having my food cut for me as well as the fine art of eating with my left hand while I nursed my oblivious little munchkin, supporting her with my right arm.

"Maternal dignity" seemed an oxymoron, but more than that, my existence became a series of newborn events that kept bringing me up short. Babies don't defer to adult schedules for many years: diapers are filled at the least opportune moments; infants sleep and wake and fuss at whim; adult urges take a backseat as the babies' tiny psyches begin to develop. For some new mothers, this randomness is part of the fun, like walking along a wilderness trail and discovering some delightfully colorful plant or animal around each turn. For others it is akin to slow torture, frustrating and depressing. For many, it is an unpredictable combination of agony and ecstasy.

New mothers experience a spectrum of reactions and emotions that have been the subject of both speculation and study. Women who have had a time of it with postpartum depression once are prone to experiencing it after subsequent deliveries as well. By administering estrogen to women with a prior history of severe postpartum depression immediately after a delivery, researchers have been able to attenuate the severity of the depressive symptoms by gradually tapering the dose of estrogen over a number of days. This phenomenon makes it look as though the abrupt postpartum rearrangement of hormones is solely responsible for postpartum blues. But this tells only part of the story. Why some women get a grip on their emotions quickly while others succumb to protracted periods of sadness and even psychosis is not understood. What is certain is that—the perinatal riptide of hormones and its influence on brain and body chemistry notwithstanding—a new mother is faced with myriad external forces and factors that can be as overwhelming and discouraging in fact as all those congratulatory cards are optimistic and uplifting in intent.

I'll never forget the scene in my hospital room the morning I took my firstborn home. I sat on the edge of the bed, crying into my cornflakes and trying to figure out how I could at once feel so happy and so sad. On the other side of the drawn curtain that separated the semiprivate room, I could hear my roommate weeping softly as well, although I never connected my sadness with hers. She must have had bad news, I thought; I, on the other hand, was just so tired. My obstetrician came and went, offering no comfort or advice but only knowing and sympathetic looks.

At the time, I was a fourth-year medical student and had paid unwavering attention to everything I was taught pertaining to obstetrics and pediatrics. I had sat with the attending physician for my psychiatry rotation trying to figure out a newborn's psychological needs. I had attended every class on bathing and feeding given by the newborn-nursery staff, then stayed to help practice what I had learned. I had eaten carefully, carried my pillow to Lamaze classes, researched infant car seats, and read everything I could get my hands on about childbirth and infant development. According to prepartum logic, I was ready.

What was missing from all my educational endeavors was any perspective on what the experience would be like for me. I knew all about the baby and almost nothing about the mother. Nothing in my training or reading had prepared me for the reality of being the primary means of another fragile entity's survival, a walking, talking chuck wagon, while at the same time being hormone central.

The version of new motherhood handed down from generation to generation, not to mention from Hollywood to viewer, anticipates that an instant and joyous bonding occurs between mother and child immediately after birth. Some women, when presented with a cone-headed, goopy, squish-faced baby, can't help giving in to a private wince. Surveying the lineup in the hospital nursery's viewing window, it may be tempting to wish that your infant resembled one of the more picture-book-looking babies. Even minor disappointment or surprise then gives way to guilt or a sense of failure right from the get go.

No one ever says, "I'd like you to meet your new child. He may not be exactly what you were anticipating, but since each baby is different, there's no telling in advance what to expect. He needs your care and attention right away, but he'll understand if it takes a little while for you to fall in love with him." Even the best of moms sometimes have to let their heads lead the way in caring for a baby while their hearts bring up the rear. The guilt this engenders exacerbates an already hormonally loaded and emotionally labile situation.

At the same time a new mom is figuring out how she feels about her baby, her perception of her husband is also undergoing a rapid metamorphosis. The expectations of equality forged by a mutually and logically agreed-upon prepartum division of labor is thrown a major curve by the arrival of a baby. Dad picks up his new son or daughter to begin his own bonding process and just as he's working up a picture-perfect look of awe and devotion, junior wails urgently and is not to be consoled by Pop. One cuddle from Mom, not to mention a suckle or two at her breast, and the baby is content—at least until Dad tries to continue his bonding efforts. In the face of this new division of labor and power, many fathers—sometimes consciously, sometimes unconsciously—begin to back away from participating in an infant's care.

During a breakout session I led a couple of years ago at a conference on the future of the family, one highly motivated and dedicated father described his experience: "I felt as though my wife and child were playing happily together behind a great wall of glass," he told the conference participants. "I could see and even hear them going merrily about their business, but they seemed to only need each other. I'd press my face up against the glass in an effort to get through to them, but they scarcely noticed me. I had to really work at not feeling resentful."

The rearrangement of allegiances that begins immediately after a baby's arrival often gives way to resentment and anger for both mother and father. Feeling excluded from the sea of change going on around them, fathers may back off, not only from their wives and offspring, but from the other domestic responsibilities they had attended to in marriage in the name of equality. Suddenly, when she most needs his help, support, and understanding, a woman may find her husband's presence, reliability, or good humor elusive. As women with postpartum depression have begun to tell their stories over the past two decades, many of them point to hostility and resentment toward their husbands as a factor in their emotional predicament. This anger stems from the perception that their partners are not willing to equally share responsibility for care of the baby or the household.

In response to all this, Mom looks happy while often feeling sad, and Dad looks competent while often feeling awkward. Because they fly in the face of the happy countenance everyone anticipates from new parents, the guilt and resentment are frequently harbored quietly. The external social expectations, based on prepartum logic, can help a couple go through the motions required by a new baby's presence, but such convictions can also get in the way of honest communication when it is most needed. That fathers and mothers experience this transformation differently is precisely the reason they need to compare notes during this time and figure out how to help each other. It is, after all—and more so even than their wedding—just the beginning.

See through the Happy Father

It was years before I realized that the ebullient energy most new fathers exhibit is generated at least as much by anxiety as it is by the mythical happiness everyone expects. The long-awaited event has taken place, the baby is being passed around for adoring relatives and friends to admire, and Dad is doing the only thing he knows how to do at the moment. He is playing out the role he has learned from watching other dads and movies; he looks happy, acts happy, sounds happy. He is the pillar. He doesn't, however, always feel the part.

Oh, sure, he is relieved to have the trauma of watching his wife go through labor behind him. And he is thrilled that the delivery went well and that his wife and infant are doing fine. Regardless of how supportive he has been throughout his partner's pregnancy, however, or how immediately connected he feels to the baby, his body remains unaffected by the process and his ability to give this baby what it wants remains limited. As a result, even though he attended every prenatal visit to the obstetrician and palpated every little kick, he is beginning to feel left out now that the birth has taken place. But he keeps smiling.

At the same time, the partner with whom he has been in this procreation thing from the beginning is suddenly and powerfully distracted from his predicament in ways that he can appreciate only at a distance. Because she remains cheerful despite having undergone labor and delivery, despite having an episiotomy, uterine pain, sore breasts, or a surgical wound from a C-section, this makes it unthinkable for him to burden her with his insecurities or concerns. A dramatic reformulation of their relationship has begun, and while he senses something is happening, she is pretty oblivious to anything but her body and the baby. Their once synchronous thoughts and dreams are starting to revolve in different spheres. Without meaning to do so, she acts as if he's some sort of emotionally bionic man. He pretends to be so and keeps on smiling.

In addition to this, everyone they know is asking about his wife and the baby. What about him? How about the fact that he is waiting on her hand and foot, that he's terrified about what they are going to do without her income for a while, that he hasn't slept in two nights, and that he never realized how unhandy he is at doing laundry. He's not sure what his role is supposed to be, what he can do right, or how he is supposed to relate to this infant. Not only that, but his mother-in-law has come to stay with them for two weeks when two days of her would be enough to drive him crazy. But he keeps smiling.

To take the edge off his worries, he goes back to work with a vengeance. He will work for two, make twice the income, provide for his wife and child. He's good at this, and besides, whenever he goes home he just moves uncomfortably between his wife who isn't her old self and his mother-in-law who is. Work is a good place to be. It's enough to help him keep on smiling.

If this is a second or third child, Dad remembers how much his existence changed when the first baby came along. Anticipatory anxiety then gets layered onto fatigue and a sense of isolation. Will the distance between his wife and him grow even greater with this new baby? Will sex ever be as frequent and carefree as it was before children? Don't think about this, he tells himself. Just keep smiling.

But he can't help it. He begins to wonder whether he and his wife will ever have sex again. The doctor advises that they wait at least until after her three-week postpartum checkup and maybe even six weeks. Three weeks would be bad enough, but six weeks! He doesn't think he'll survive. But then he remembers . . . there is this new baby to think of, and really, this baby needs him in ways that he's quite sure will become apparent as time goes on. If he had a good relationship with his own father, his faith in this eventuality will bolster him during this transition. If not, it may add to his emotional anguish that nobody seems to notice because he is doing such a good job of imitating all the other happy fathers he's ever seen. He knows that for the time being he should just keep on smiling.

All this smiling serves an admirable purpose: it helps keep familial peace at a time when peace is greatly needed. The new father who can set aside his own needs in the interest of his new or newly enlarged family is performing an indispensable labor of love. In the midst of this, however, the new mother who can see past the facial expression to some of her husband's angst and let him know that she appreciates what he's going through will have reached out at a crucial time. Mutual compassion and support during this time will help head off misunderstandings and resentments later. A kind word here and there between partners will go a long way toward keeping everyone—Mom, Dad, and Baby—smiling and together.

Bob and Weave

The tenuous, complex play of emotions that comprises new parenthood gives way to subtle, then not-so-subtle behavioral changes. Feminism, whether a fully operative notion in a given relationship or not, defined equality for all post-sixties generations of women and, by association, men. My peers came into motherhood believing unwaveringly in equality of everything: pay, vacation, status, libido, doing household chores, and—before offspring were a fait accompli—attachment to children. Our consuming ideology flew in the face of dividing labor, whether domestic or otherwise, according to gender. The biological realities we faced when our nursing babies preferred our touch, smell, and lullabies to our husbands' required an uncomfortable retreat to an era we thought we had so handily left behind. Teamwork had meant becoming fluent and accomplished in all professional and domestic matters and walking in step, not dividing labor, the way our parents had, according to what came most easily to each partner. Yet something about that baby made us willing to chuck the single standard or at least a hefty chunk of it.

No one was ever more devoted to medicine than I was in my prepartum incarnation. At home with my new baby and with my husband back in his office, however, I couldn't read a medical journal or seem to much care about health issues beyond those referable to my healing episiotomy and sore breasts and those having direct bearing on my baby. My husband was back at it, writing prescriptions, making brilliant diagnoses, and having lunch and good conversation at the hospital with our colleagues. I, meanwhile, was furiously pumping and freezing breast milk in anticipation of my return to work, fretting about the color and texture of newborn stools, and abandoning my morning shower with but one leg shaved at the slightest peep of discontentment from the baby. My husband would arrive home after work to the sight of me dressed in his clothes (roomier in the waist), trying to make dinner with the baby strapped in a front pack. Fortunately, we had learned enough from TV sitcoms to offer a mutual, "Hi, honey. How was your day?" whether we really wanted to hear about the other's activities or not.

Little by little our expectations of each other changed. He had little interest in diapering, comforting, or devoting himself to the baby for more than brief periods of time. I had little interest in doing anything else. At first, however, we were in sufficient denial about what was happening to keep acting the way we had before, even if we were no longer sure how to feel. When I returned to the hospital to finish my medical school clerkships, I suspect my husband heaved a sigh of relief, thinking he'd have the old me back once my professional context was reestablished. The truth is that I was never my old self again. Motherhood changes too many things.

Perhaps the pivotal point in the postpartum dance is what happens to the respective libidos of new parents. Joseph Campbell called libido the impulse to life, a concept that tells the tale of new parents. Childbirth redirects that impulse for a new mother. The baby wields the baton, conducting maternal impulses unrelentingly. Physically, hormonally, and emotionally, however, a new father has not changed, or if he has, the change is externally motivated. He may heel to a higher level of responsibility in caring for the baby, but his fundamental identity hasn't changed as profoundly as has his partner's—at least at first. Even fathers who decide to stay home to be their children's primary caregiver, while grappling with a new identity, haven't undergone the same psychophysiological alterations that impact new moms. Testosterone still surges in the same way it did before fatherhood and with it, sexual desire. It doesn't take long for new parents to begin to newly appreciate and understand—if uncomfortably— all the jokes they've ever heard about sex and married couples.

Faced with the incontrovertible given that men and women experience childbirth differently, a woman's allegiances begin to shift and become divided. Suddenly she is sleep-deprived a good part of the time; while breast feeding continues, her hormones are still in flux; if labor was difficult or surgery required, she is on the mend for a time. Her full attention, her impulse to life, is riveted on her newborn. In this situation, many women are unable to locate their prior interest in sex for some time after giving birth. This can reinforce feelings of guilt, it can add a layer to any existing resentment when husbands don't understand, or it can be taken underground in an effort to maintain an even keel in the relationship. In any event, it can be disconcerting for both partners.

Although certain themes emerge from the process of going from a couple to a family, no two couples are alike. For various reasons, some women are uncomfortable nursing or caring for infants, a reality that sends them back to work as soon as possible. Other women cannot financially afford an extensive maternity leave or may be more highly motivated by their professional situations than by mothering and also return to work posthaste. These days, most women attempt to find some happy medium between their work and home lives, although the happy part can be eclipsed by trying to do too many things at once.

The stories are as varied for men as for women. Not all men have difficulty finding their fathering legs. While it often takes a verbal child to bring out the best in a dad, more and more fathers are picking up the parenting ball right from the start. Seventeen percent of families, we are told, now have fathers at the homemaking helm while their wives are the primary breadwinners. My colleagues in undertaking family formation in the 1970s and 1980s had only theory to rely on when it came to forging equitable mother-father arrangements. Subsequent generations have actually been able to build on the tried—if not always true—stay-at-home or go-to-work formulas we concocted. More young men are coming of age with fathers at home (not a whole lot mind you, but some), which may create more choice for women than did thirty years of ideological rumination. But mutating the domestic gender-role arrangement is evolutionarily slow and may take even longer than the reflective approach.

Creativity has become the name of the game in the emotion-packed transition from life before baby to life ever after. And while a primary model of the American family no longer exists—as it did, say, in the 1950s and 1960s—the brunt of homemaking still falls to women. Men who mash bananas, dads who develop baby-sitter lists, husbands who house-clean, and fathers who fathom sick kids are still, after all this time, the exception rather than the rule. Yet research indicates that in most situations, as fathers become more involved in home responsibilities, not only do women and children benefit, but the men themselves find the involvement rewarding and satisfying. This may explain why an increasing number of men who become stay-at-home dads for even a brief time are finding themselves so enlightened that they are writing whole books about the same experiences women have ho-hummed for centuries.

Societal inflexibility and workplace demands are often cited as presenting the greatest obstacles to becoming a parentally ambidextrous family. These factors require the person who can make the most money in the shortest time—most often the man—to assume the breadwinning position. But other more subtle hurdles crop up as partners in family formation cast about to define their roles in the postpartum setting. One of these is many new mothers' reluctance to unconditionally consign the baby's care to their partner—except, perhaps, episodically. Being able to watch someone else, even Dad, do things differently where baby is concerned is next to impossible for some women. This, of course, adds insult to alienation from Dad's point of view, and he asks himself, "Why bother?"

When *la différence* rears its irritable and unpredictable head during the first year of new parenthood, the fitness of the original match is called upon to steady the relationship. A good match not only will have survived the perinatal interval but will have found new dimensions to its strength during this period that will come home with the baby. The relationship can never be exactly the same as it was before children, and it may not be "better" in any definable way, but it has more at stake. Parents who have traveled the distance from childbirth to college tuition often wonder what keeps childless couples together over the long haul without the glue that children squeeze into a marriage's cracks and chips.

In addition to each partner's fundamental suitability for the marriage, other factors mitigate the tricky times that a baby's addition often elicit. The ability to trust the marriage's soundness as it is redefined, as the notion of romance molts and acquires new trappings, can take a couple a long way. Knowing how important both partners are to a child's psychosocial development can inspire a cooperative approach to stressful times. Just keeping a sense of humor when things don't go as planned can single-handedly save a marriage. And the ability to bob and weave, to learn new dance steps to new music—shared music, family music, music for three or more—is a skill all new parents would do well to cultivate. But as the new feminists have discovered, it takes two to tango.

Hear Your Heart, Use Your Head

It is not enough that a new mom has to decipher what her baby wants from her while simultaneously renegotiating her marital terrain. No, even when she is making good headway on those fronts, she finds herself alternately encouraged and daunted by what everyone else expects from her. As her maternity leave winds down, the questions are no longer as simple as which wallpaper should grace the nursery or what to fix for dinner. Things have gotten a bit more complicated.

Her employer calls to congratulate her and is, while he's got her on the phone and completely parenthetically mind you, just curious about when she might be back on the job. If she has clients, they send gifts and flowers and inundate her with congratulatory phone calls. After, "What did you name her?" however, they want to know when she'll be getting to their project and offer to drop it off or pick it up if that would be convenient. Perhaps they could do lunch.

Still, everyone else's expectations are only one aspect of what confounds a new mom's honest soul search. Unsolicited judgments abound. Even maternal grandmothers, the mothers of the mothers, who as founts of firsthand experience should be most sympathetic, or at least sensitive, to their own daughters' postpartum adjustments, don't seem to recollect anything about having a baby. What Grandma may remember too well are things like what she paid for her daughter's college or graduate degrees, or that she meant it when she offered to take care of the baby when her daughter returns to work, or how much she always wished she had had the professional opportunities her daughter has had.

Or perhaps Grandma represents the old school and is continually taken aback when her daughter mentions resuming a professional life. She may chatter endlessly about how being a mother was the center of her existence, how it was career enough, and, she might add, how well her daughter turned out because of it. She might even offer to help out with finances if that would take her daughter's mind off the unthinkable— leaving the grandbaby with a perfect stranger.

Even when, anxiety and second-guessing notwithstanding, a woman has made up her mind about what she wants or has to do, the tumult continues. She picks up a magazine in her obstetrician's waiting room as she awaits her six-week postpartum checkup and reads of professional women who return to the nest to nuzzle and live happily ever after with their new babies, stitching quilts and running bake sales for good causes. When our new mom is ushered into the exam room, she pages through another magazine, a glitzy offering, featuring an impeccably dressed and coifed CEO who, the interview reports, exercises for an hour each morning before leaving her tastefully decorated home for her highly paid job. She is pictured with her adoring husband, three perfectly gorgeous kids, and the family's golden retriever, all hovering around Mom at her desk. Even the dog is smiling.

Our new mom is discouraged. She stops in the waiting room again on her way out to nurse her now fussy infant. While she does this, a well-put-together woman with slightly greying hair, accompanied by a teenage daughter, comes over to admire the baby. "You're so lucky," this woman tells our mom. "There is nothing as precious as a little one. Enjoy her because she'll be grown and gone before you know it." The teenager rolls her eyes at her mother's comment, but smiles sweetly at the baby. Our new mom, hiding the fact that she is now overcome with conflicting emotions, thanks this woman for her kind comments, nods pleasantly at the girl, then gathers her belongings and heads to the parking lot.

On the drive home, the baby falls asleep in her car seat and our new mom is listening to a therapist's call-in radio show. A harried mother is on the line to ask advice about juggling her new child and her job, but the therapist cuts her off midsentence. This mother is advised that she has no business "juggling" her baby but should be figuring out how she or her husband can stay home with the baby until he starts school. Our new mom finds herself staring at the radio until her own baby begins to whimper, reminding her that she has stopped for a red light that has now turned green.

Arriving home, our new mom checks the mail only to find a pile of bills. She is reminded that her maternity leave has already exhausted the small cash reserve she and her husband had managed to accumulate in anticipation of her time away from work. It doesn't help that several of these bills are for payments on money she borrowed for her graduate school tuition, money that was going to be a drop in the bucket compared to her ability to earn.

How, she wonders to herself, could she not have had a clue that things were never going to be as simple as she and her husband had planned? How did she come to be thirty years old without knowing that becoming a mother would change her perspective on things? Why didn't her husband seem to be rearranging his priorities too? What was she going to do?

Just then the phone rings. When she says hello, our new mom is greeted by a friend who apologizes for calling her at home, but has a pressing issue about which she needs some quick professional advice. Balancing the baby over one shoulder while cradling the receiver in the other, our new mom spends the next ten minutes discussing her friend's concern then exchanges a little small talk. After hanging up she inexplicably feels much better. There is a world out there that values her professional talents; this phone call has reminded her of the satisfaction she gets from her job.

The task before her, then, is one that neither the conservative nor progressive incarnation of her mother could know. It is not one that her employer, clients, colleagues, or any magazine article can solve for her. And it is not one that abides the inflexibility of a talk-show host pitching a black-or-white moralistic gimmick. Her dilemma is uniquely hers. Her maternal instincts, financial situation, husband's job, child's health and particular needs, available benefits, and own job will define a solution that other people may envy or criticize, but won't have to live with. Her heart and head will forge a plan that may work at first and come up short later but will—and this she needs to remember—always be reworkable. Whatever arrangement she makes will not be cast in stone.

Raise Your Child Wisely and the Village Will Prosper

Ever since some resourceful commentator called upon what is now a commonly known old African saying to make a gracious point, the appeal of this adage, not to mention its political overtones, has made it a hot topic of conversation during the nineties. "It takes a village to raise a child" is a lovely sentiment by anyone's standards, but is much more naive than it sounds. The "village," for instance, has given us our deteriorating public education system; welfare; racism; the need for V-chips on televisions to screen out nudity, violence, and profanity; and pedophilia on the Internet. There is, make no mistake, a downside to relying too trustingly upon the village. It is safer to trust that it takes good parents to raise a village.

In our ruggedly individualistic society, the village is the flimsiest of safety nets. Our village elders are too bogged down in political allegiances to be of real help to the folks who most need it. Moreover, in our heterogeneous culture, village values are a little like garage sale items: one family's trash is another family's treasure. Even the basics, the provisions of the Constitution and the Bill of Rights, are the subject of political disagreements. What, for instance, did the founding fathers intend when they codified the right of an individual to bear arms? Could it be that at a time when local militias constituted a community's only defense, gun ownership had a patriotic purpose, a purpose that has long since become anachronistic, self-defeating, and in many instances downright unpatriotic?

The village sometimes seems to have outgrown its capacity to act in its own best interest and has devolved, like so many unhappy siblings wanting their "fair" share, into a state of chronic bickering: new math or new new math; welfare or workfare; affirmative action or the best, the brightest, and the racist; choice or religious concretism; censorship or wildly free speech; parents or village. Without a guiding or obvious principle upon which to decide our conflicts, and in the absence of unbought or objective elders, the answer had better come from the parent.

The concept of the village working together to benefit the child depended on certain village adults having time available to assist children besides their own. In *Wait Till Next Year*, her heartwarming memoir of growing up on Long Island during the fifties, Harvard historian Doris Kearns Goodwin describes what life was like for children when most mothers were home during the day and children moved freely from one house to another. Although Goodwin's mother was often sickly and could not tolerate much activity, Goodwin nonetheless had a kindly reservoir of adults throughout the neighborhood to encourage and watch over her.

The dark side of the fifties, which tacitly confined women to their homes, has been explored in great detail since the early days of feminism. The positives of having parents around the village when children are home got left out of the discussions that eventually reconfigured the family. Now, when a parent calls a friend to ask for help, it is with the knowledge that everyone is time-pressed and overextended. In this setting, small favors that were once unnoticeable in the village take on the flavor of major impositions, and the burden inevitably trickles down to those necessitating the favors—the kids.

Still, in our imperfect village where it's mainly every family for itself, some parents are, by virtue of income or situation, clearly in control of helping shape their children's destinies. Other parents, precisely because of this peculiar autonomy, could use a little constructive assistance. Until now, this assistance has been a top-down proposition, the remedial efforts coming after something has gone awry. It seems so obvious that nipping problems in the bud is far more effective than trying to solve them after they've become established. Any drug-enforcement official knows this. Rather than waiting until after the teen pregnancy has occurred; the marriage is on the rocks; or the child is having difficulty in school, has begun smoking cigarettes, or has been abused—rather than trying to fix what is decidedly broken—the village could offer early parental education and prevent at least some fraction of the noxious problems that describe these vicious societal and generational circles.

The village's power, like a parent's power, lies in its ability to attach a few strings. We will, the village elders might say to a family, provide vouchers so you can send your kids to good—we mean really good—preschools. That way you won't have to leave your children every morning at a place that makes you nervous, a place where you suspect they watch television all day, but which is all you can afford. In return, you parents—both of you—need to attend an hour (or two or three) of parent-education classes each week. The win-win here is a real deal. The kids get what every child should have, not day care but good early childhood education, and the mother and father get what every set of parents should have—parenting education.

The voucher system has been suggested time and again as a cure for the ills of the public school system. For the most part, however, it has too vividly threatened the status quo. Speculation abounds on this subject. It is said that vouchers will ghettoize the public schools, polarize ethnic groups, violate tenets concerning the separation of church and state, help the rich get richer, and ring the death knell for the universal, melting pot, multi-ethnic public education we've come to know and that forms the basis of our democratic system. In truth, no one will ever know how vouchers would impact the system until they are tried. Because it wouldn't require restructuring an enormous extant system, because of the voluntary nature of early childhood education, and because it is an area in dire need of attention, preschool might be the perfect place to try out educational vouchers.

Lots of other areas beg for attention when it comes to helping parents help their kids. Front-end (rather than the chronic rear-end) marital counseling with periodic refresher sessions, ongoing parenting education, easy access to birth control, and continued income when there is a bona fide need for a parent to be home on family leave—all of these could be made available. When parents have the tools to give their children optimal educations and the prospect of better things to come, a sense of hope replaces the despair that otherwise spirals downward into sad family stories. The key is to leave parents in control of the specifics while giving them an opportunity to make good choices. In this scenario the parents, children, and family are not the only beneficiaries; the village, in the long run, will have raised itself.

Educate Your Fantasies

In anticipating their lives as wives and mothers, it's easy for most women to imagine having babies. Despite being rife with myths about happy fathers or sex always being a mutual pursuit, the landscape of life with little ones is comfortably conjured. Moreover, an enormous body of literature, an astounding number of organizations, a plethora of gizmos, and an impressive amount of lore exist to help a woman navigate the early years of motherhood. Glaring gaps in guidance notwithstanding, there's something about having small children around that keeps the fantasies alive, optimism at hand, and energy flowing.

Perhaps because they tend not to be the stuff of which daydreams are spun, the unexpected eventualities always come as a surprise. Things like sick children, infirm relatives, stepchildren, and teenagers don't take on even a pastel presence in anticipatory meditations; they don't figure in at all when a woman contemplates growing old with her chosen partner. Yet some or all of these things inevitably go bump in the night, and often, like most other aspects of a domestic or personal nature, more noticeably invade a woman's sphere than her husband's.

Coming upon the unexpected may be as precipitous as getting a phone call from school saying your child has fallen from the play structure and is in the emergency room. More often, however, it's a little like being a kid by a pool; you're in the middle of it before you realize you don't know how to swim. When I consider the early years of my marriage, it reminds me of that pool and although I knew how to swim, I didn't know how to carry someone else on my back in the water.

When I met my husband, he had a three-year-old daughter from a previous marriage that ended when this little girl was not yet two. Because he was conscientious about having his daughter visit as often as possible, the time he and I spent together naturally included a fair amount of time as a threesome. I was young then and about as clueless as they come. I became very fond of this little girl for a number of reasons, not the least of which were that she was very bright and lovable and that she came with the guy. I never wondered how she would figure in my future because the idea was that we'd all just live happily ever after. At our wedding she was the flower girl opposite my nephew, the ring bearer, and fantasy flowed.

Less than a year after that, I had my first child and everything changed. I was trying to finish medical school, worrying about my residency, commuting between the coasts, and just barely keeping my own baby, body, and soul together. My stepdaughter in all her innocence bounced in and out of the picture as she always had. Gradually, without my understanding this on a conscious level, this little girl became a symbol to me of any frustration I had with my husband during this time. Suddenly, through no fault of hers, she was an icon of my disappointment that my husband wasn't as fully engaged by our baby as I expected him to be. It wasn't that he wouldn't change a diaper or carry the baby in a front pack; it was just that his excitement about the entire experience didn't seem to match mine. This was my first glimpse of the differences between how men approach fatherhood and women motherhood. Then too, because he had been through it all before, parenthood didn't hold the novelty for my husband that it did for me.

Why I shifted my disenchantment to my stepdaughter is anybody's guess. A psychologist once pointed out that the happily-ever-after fantasies with which little girls are raised don't include stepchildren. What this means for adult women is that at some really base level, stepmothers wish their stepchildren didn't exist because these kids get in the way of the nuclear-family fantasy. Never mind that plenty else gets in the way either first or eventually. Stepchildren, however, are there from the start as convenient objects of transference; a new wife or mother transfers her dissatisfaction with her husband directly onto the unsuspecting stepkids. Some stepchildren inadvertently facilitate this process by reacting negatively to it. My stepdaughter, though, just kept on being her delightful self and never gave up trying to get back the relationship she and I had enjoyed before she was displaced by my own children. Even as a child, she had much better instincts about the situation than I did as an adult.

This is a common story, albeit a sad one. Studies repeatedly indicate that men have an easier time being stepfathers than women do being stepmothers. And although I can think of about a zillion reasons why this might be the case, it remains unfortunate for the kids. A piece of the solution to this problem inevitably lies in drawing men more fully into the domestic realm and the caretaking roles that women predominantly fill. When men are gladly, enthusiastically, easily, and comfortably taking care of all their own children, then women—whether step- or biological moms—will be more than glad to join the fun. But when this happens, there will also be fewer stepchildren to get caught between families.

In looking back on the quandary into which I stumbled early in my marriage, I've often wondered how I might have seen things more clearly. Who should or could have told me what was coming? My mother had never had stepchildren; my husband, like me, was hoping for the best; my friends were no better informed than I. Perhaps the marriage-license clerk could have asked, however routinely, "Are there any children involved?" Then to my affirmative reply, she would have slapped two pamphlets on the counter and said, "One for you, one for your fiancé. You'll both need to sign a statement acknowledging you've read the information before I can issue your marriage license."

What would those pamphlets contain? At least study results, likelihoods, true stories, psychological insights, and suggestions about stepfamilies. Information of that sort would have helped on any number of counts, but whereas I had plenty of time to get used to the other issues that confounded my fantasies, stepparenthood was as imminent as the marriage and bore illuminating immediately.

Most licenses are issued after a training period or at least after some sort of understanding is reached about a situation. In preparation to drive, my oldest daughter recently completed many hours of classroom instruction and supervised behind-the-wheel experience and has next to demonstrate, by being tested, a knowledge of the rules of and competence on the road. And while it is unlikely that a test will ever be required prior to the issuance of a marriage license, it wouldn't hurt to put a little information in place as a prerequisite. Given the loaded nature of that information from a political, religious, and cultural point of view, however, the most a marriage license is ever likely to demonstrate is that a couple can afford the fee.

Nonetheless, some fundamental stones could be turned over for individuals before the marriage ceremony rather than afterward. And whereas I could have set out to educate myself about stepparenting, I was sufficiently ignorant and naive on the subject that I wouldn't have known where to begin. The Catholic Church, among others, is pretty good at making couples attend premarital counseling sessions, but because the Catholic Church has a few fantasies of its own, they do this primarily to ensure that any children resulting from the union will be added to the ranks of little Catholics. A secular effort in a similar vein, not to proselytize but to inform, would be a worthy addition to our current marriage licensing system—it could go along with those coupons for periodic marital counseling. You need not demonstrate any expertise in raising stepchildren as Catholics, just as kids. Information could only help. Knowledge, after all and as the T-shirt says, is power, and ignorance within the context of a marriage is definitely not bliss.

Opening parental eyes to an issue, or heads to the facts, doesn't guarantee that hearts will open as a result. Still, if couples could wrap their mutual fantasies around a little reality in advance of a marriage, it might make it easier to embrace some of the things that are bound, sooner or later, to lead to regrets or to make the unanticipated go bump in the night.

Chapter Three

Choices Must Be Made, Prices Must Be Paid

The strongest principle of growth lies in human choice.
—George Eliot

W hile all mothers work, some—in fact, most these days—need to work for income as well as for their families. Aside from how much income is required, many variables will contribute to the individual balance a woman strikes between home and work. Styles of marital collaboration, number and ages of children, how circumstances change over time, and the availability, cost, and quality of child care all influence an infinite number of solutions to the work-family dilemma. And while a solution may serve magnificently for a period of time or for one woman, that same solution may lose its utility later on or not suffice at all for another mother. Each choice made in forging a particular work-family equilibrium has its pluses and minuses. The best any mother can do for herself and her family is take her cues from unique, personal considerations rather than from someone else's answers or ideology.

Compose Your Own Story

Growing up with feminism created some underlying assumptions for many women and men about what marriage would be like. Mutual lip service was usually accorded the place of children within the union, but beyond that women anticipated one thing and men another. Women saw boundless freedom to pursue their dreams with men as true helpmates; men saw, as one friend of mine likes to put it, "tits and dollar signs." In other words, women looked forward to being all their mothers never were, and men looked forward to liberated sex and help bringing home the bacon. As these very different sets of expectations merged after the vows, they predicted—still predict—the course of a marriage.

In many instances, the chasm between these expectations in the initial aftermath of a marriage is bridged by a number of sustaining influences: common interests; the continuation of frequent, creative, attentive "courtship" sex; youthful energy; and a lack of significant time pressures. Often this bridge doesn't begin to show wear and tear until it has to support the weight of children, at which point some reengineering is in order. Some couples are able to do this and some are not. Many just keep dodging the bridge's weak points and hoping that a few snapped cables won't make it impassable.

There are a number of ways to reengineer this bridge between differing expectations, provided a couple looks to solve problems within the context of their particular relationship. It does no good to compare your situation to that of a friend who may have more money, fewer children, an older spouse, or any of the jillion variables that give each marriage a unique fingerprint. Besides, no one really knows what goes on behind closed doors in a marriage; the couple who looks ideal may have a relationship as fraught with emotional pain as any other. Stick to reengineering your own bridge.

Letting go of some of the presumptions you brought to the marriage may be the first and most difficult step in this process. This doesn't mean letting go of what is important to you, compromising your values, or even being disappointed. It may, however, mean changing your expectations as circumstances change. If, for instance, I had gone through my marriage feeling bitter about not having been able to become a top-notch vascular surgeon, I would either be single by now, or a miserable person to live with, or both. My premotherhood ambitions, however, were incompatible with having a growing family, a career, and a driven husband. This didn't become apparent all at once, either to me or my husband. Gradually, though, as our responsibilities increased, we each gravitated to the tasks and roles with which we were comfortable and at which we were most adept. The end result has been a far more traditional marriage than either of us ever anticipated twenty years ago, but one that has made ample room for children and the rewards that come with raising them.

Moreover, what some might see as the constraints of motherhood have actually presented me with opportunities. I don't view the professional path I've taken as strewn with sacrifices, but rather as being full of interesting challenges. Instead of going to an office and laying my hands on ten or twenty patients each day, I've spent less time and reached more people by writing about parenting and preventative health care for newspapers and magazines during times when office or clinic work was impractical. There are many ways to use a medical degree including research, office practice, medical administration, and education. Had I not had children, I might never have looked beyond the commonplace versions of how to be a physician. While combining other talents and interests with medicine, motherhood—aside from being the main incentive—has provided layers of experience and perspective that would be hard to come by any other way.

At the same time, my husband and I require ongoing negotiations to modify our expectations about who is going to bring home how much bacon and who is going to attend to the various unpaid jobs that need doing. And, unsurprisingly, each time we thought we had a workable arrangement, something always changed. It bodes well when the ability to bob and weave becomes a synchronous and collective skill in a marriage.

There are innumerable ways to address the work-family dilemma that inevitably appears once children arrive on the scene. These tend to fall into one of five categories: very traditional, modified traditional, equal standing, modified reverse, and reverse traditional. With the mass movement of women into the workplace, the very traditional arrangements of the fifties in which the woman tends the kids and home front exclusively while Dad provides the income are becoming increasingly scarce. At the same time, the modified version of this, in which the woman works part-time and handles domestic affairs while Dad works full-time, has become very common. Marriages in which gainful employment and attention to domestic matters are shared equally are less prevalent, but the other two situations, those in which the father takes up most or all of the home work while the mom brings home the bulk of the bacon are on the rise.

What's important in considering options for marital collaboration is that the individual circumstances and participants be honored. The birth of a disabled child will throw a wrench into a marriage of equal standing. A traditional marriage will have to be rearranged if either the mother's or father's health deteriorates. And a modified traditional marriage will often become more traditional with the arrival of each additional child. Just the matter of staying together over years and years will indelibly change the contour of any marriage.

Despite the one-sidedness of the feminist push to establish equal pay for equal work, it managed to bring domestic issues along in at least one respect. It is now well accepted that women and men can both earn income, manage households, and tend children. Whether that cultural acceptance will ever translate into widespread equality in matters of practical life is anybody's guess. In the meantime, it is up to each couple to negotiate the collaborative scheme that best fits their own needs, then keep on negotiating as time revises the original scenario and the learning curve enlightens the future.

Believe What You See

Despite the wisdom of doing so, many of us did not have the foresight to establish ourselves preeminently in our professions before becoming mothers. Even those who did, however, did not possess any magical ability to cope with their dual roles or ignore the conflicts that inevitably arose. No matter how smart or rich or well organized, most professional moms struggle with the push-pull of knowing what their kids need as opposed to what their jobs require.

Unfortunately, most information about how to be gainfully employed and still be a good mom contains a current of conservative, retro information. There are working moms out there who have moved their professional goals to a later point in life and who make other working moms feel bad about not staying home while their children are little. "I stayed home with my little one," they say on radio talk shows and in syndicated columns. "So should you." Aside from the obvious arrogance of this position, this sort of backlash theory is just plain bad advice when issued as a blanket statement.

One of the many deficiencies of the backlash against feminism is that, in reacting to the foibles of the original feminist philosophy, it goes to the opposite extreme. Rather than honestly undertaking a search for a useful happy medium that would allow women to realize their career goals or lifelong dreams without foregoing motherhood, the wanna-be backlash ideologists have set up a new either-or situation. By attempting to convince women that irreparable psychological, if not physical, harm will surely come to children who don't have full-time moms, these new militants have created an ideology at least as naive as the original stick-'em-in-child-care feminism.

For decades doctors have known that a child's experiences in his first two or three years of life set the stage emotionally and intellectually for what comes later. To be sure, consistency, predictability, and safety seem to be key elements contributing to a child's sense of security. Moreover, given a healthy set of parents, no one will look out for a child's well-being more tenaciously than those parents.

Yet outcomes are so much more complicated than these simple tenets predict. Any reliable measure of cause and effect about who cares for a child, how, for how long, and when is confounded innumerable times before a down-the-line result can be tested. Indeed, some infants may be substantially better off with a baby-sitter than with a conflicted, frustrated full-time mom—which is not to say that a mother who thrives on external gratification should not have a baby.

Although long-term outcomes are difficult to assess, work's effects on mothers and infants has been considered in great detail. The majority of these studies demonstrate that, within certain parameters, when the child care is good and the woman enjoys her work, the net effect is beneficial to both Baby and Mom. For example, one study that looked at three- to six-year-olds, found that staying at home during the early years was only beneficial for mothers who ended up with routine, humdrum jobs later on. When mothers had challenging, interesting jobs, children showed adverse effects if the mothers did not go back to work soon. This same study went on to show, however, that when mothers or fathers worked a significant amount of overtime, the children were more at risk for problems, and the best outcomes for children resulted when mothers worked twenty to thirty-four hours per week.

As with any study of small children, there is room to wiggle. The methods, the developmental markers looked at, the individual variations in home and childcare situations, the children's young age, and their varying personalities and temperaments make it difficult to extrapolate from this study in sweeping generalizations. Common sense, however, tells us that hoards of well-adjusted, bright kids do well, some exceptionally well, after experiencing surrogate care while they were very young.

Psychological theories come and go. The entire underpinning of modern psychology rests on Freud's work, which is now, bit by not-pretty bit, being debunked. Autism was once thought to be the result of inadequate mothering which, it turns out, has nothing to do with autism. Bed-wetting used to be blamed on bad parenting which, it turns out, has nothing to do with bed-wetting. Obsessive-compulsive disorder was once attributed to some experiential adversity which, it turns out, has little if anything to do with obsessive-compulsive disorder. The complexities of child rearing, by virtue of being resistant to completely objective testing, have always been fertile ground wherein to lay blame for less than perfect outcomes. The ultimate drawback to the backlash ideology on this topic lies in the inevitability that there is no such thing as a perfect outcome.

Just looking at the generations, like mine, who had the supposed benefit of full-time mothers is enough to convince anyone that dedicated maternal caregiving is but one of many factors influencing—not necessarily positively—the character, personality development, and psychological stability an individual carries into adulthood. Witness middle-aged baby boomers' staggering demand for antidepressant medication and therapy, and rest assured that even though, as kids, their fifties and sixties moms awakened them from morning naps to tiny bologna sandwiches and bowls of Campbell's soup, they cannot now testify to an outcome-based soundness of having full-time mothers.

But there is more to the discussion about whether to leave a small child in surrogate care than just a defense of the working mom. The child-development data increasingly points to the very early years of a child's life as being critical to how he or she eventually learns, hopes, copes, and performs. Perhaps because preschool represents such a digression from the way things were done in the first half of this century, or because it took educational systems a while to recognize the challenge and opportunity of having younger students to teach, or maybe even because women are polarized on the subject—whatever the reason, we persist to this day in referring to most away-from-home situations for children as "child care." The better settings, the ones we should be making available to all kids, are really centers for early childhood education. When they do their job well, their tiny students have an advantage over most children who stay at home until starting kindergarten or first grade.

From the time they were eighteen months old, my kids had Montessori school and its sandpaper letters and pink towers to stimulate their reading and math development. But factors other than their formal schooling influenced their love of learning in my absences. They—and I—had great baby-sitters.

From the time she was eight months old, my youngest, Francesca, had Laurel. Not only did Laurel share her fondness for music, art, and movement with Francesca, but Laurel's boyfriend (now husband) was the lead singer in a rock group. Wherever Laurel went, music and dancing followed. During this time another sitter, Adriana, came every Saturday and tickled the ivories of our old upright piano. To this day, Francesca plays the piano almost effortlessly and loves nothing better than to dance, dance, dance.

My second oldest daughter, Madeleine, may have paid more attention to Laurel's boyfriend than to Laurel. Some years later, as a direct result of his influence—albeit much to our neighbors' consternation—Madeleine took up playing the drums, and for the last two years has held down the rhythm section in her junior high school jazz band.

Then there was Heather, whose knowledge of animal husbandry rubbed off on the kids and the bunny population in our backyard. When my daughter Vanessa had to observe a professional for a day in seventh grade, Heather's gone-but-not-forgotten guidance may have come back to her: Vanessa chose to spend the day with our family veterinarian.

And I am reasonably certain that Vanessa would not enjoy art as much as she does were it not for her first nanny, Leslie, who came to live with us when Vanessa was a year-and-a-half old. Leslie's patience, imagination, and artistic talent led my daughter in directions my matter-of-fact approach would never have traveled. Later, when she was three, Vanessa's extraordinary art teacher engaged her already primed creativity and took it to new heights. As I write this, Vanessa, now fifteen, has assembled ten young children in our garage for a summer art camp. She didn't get this from me; she was fortunate enough to have me work.

Believe What You Feel

There comes a time for many working mothers when full-time work begins to exact a price they are not willing to pay. Some mothers, in fact, reach a point when any work away from home becomes impractical. Even ardent workaholics have been known to step back from their obsessive tendencies in response to the catch-22 of trying to dovetail their work's inflexible schedule with their children's unpredictable demands.

This happens in as many ways as there are women making the transition from full-time work. While some seem to have crystal balls and appear to stay one step ahead of the stress monster, others capitulate to domesticity only after having been chased screaming through the streets of sanity and cornered with no possibility of escape from the monster's fiery breath. The most common complaint I hear from the working mothers among my patients is that they feel chronically overwhelmed.

Still, the contingent of women who stay home with children often talk apologetically about their decision. A sense of having copped out plagues them, as does an inferiority complex about their status in life. I've come and gone from medicine several times over the past fifteen years, and every time I step back from practicing, I feel like I've let someone down. Having been programmed during feminism's heyday, I worry about not doing my share of the breadwinning, I cringe about having taken up a place in medical school and not giving back the way a guy would, and I appreciate my patients' frustration when they can't get long-term continuity of care from me.

Sheer realism has conquered all these anxieties. I finally came to grips with the fact that my husband will never ferret out a child's soccer jersey and make sure it's clean for the game that starts in two hours. He is, and not just by my estimation, an extremely talented physician. He was not, however, raised with large doses of practical-life wisdom and has little experience, and probably more to the point little interest, in cooking, household maintenance, and overseeing children's lives and schedules. And while I struggled with this for years before I accepted the notion that everyone was happier when he did what he did best and I did the rest, my roles provide me a flexibility and versatility I treasure. I can, after all, be a mother and a physician and do more or less of each as is demanded of me.

An extinct part of my brain used to believe that being with my kids wasn't as honorable—whatever that meant—as practicing medicine. This inferiority center died off slowly as the learning process of mothering proceeded. The only thing wrong with being a full-time mom is that it isn't appropriately reimbursed, a societal derangement I have to live with, but I don't have to validate. I occasionally get a glimpse of how things really work, as I did once from a colleague with whom I trained during my internship. This woman had two small sons at the time and had never taken more than a few weeks away from medicine. I had always imagined that she shook her head at my semiabandonment of medicine every time I had a baby. Nonetheless, when I announced my intention to resume practicing two years after my fourth child was born, she sounded disappointed. She said she had been hoping I would "hold out" and that she had always admired the priority I placed on my family.

Some women, caught in the bind that motherhood places on working schedules, find ways to keep up the appearance of working full-time after they've cut way back or of working part-time when they've stopped altogether. I see this everywhere, a friend of mine being just one example. A lawyer and mother of three, she confided to me one day that, although she tries to keep her professional commitments to twenty hours per week in order to accommodate her kids' needs, she would never want a judge or client to discover this. The arrangement she has forged for herself speaks loudly, not only to the brief distance our culture has come in accepting any but the old male rendition of professional commitment, but to the things women will do to keep up appearances. My friend rents an office in a large law firm where her shingle is displayed, her telephone calls handled, and an illusion maintained that she is always available. In reality, she maintains a solo practice and limits her hours significantly. In describing this arrangement, my friend lowered her voice as though she might be found out. This is the same obeisance required by the old order of many a professional working mom.

We've come to this point in the name of progress, although headway can often be difficult to discern. Women who feel trapped between the rock of work and the hard place of home are often those who are unhappily employed, get little help at home from their partners, or are financially strapped. In combination, these stressors can wear down even the most upbeat women. Some women, however, have no option and are financially compelled to keep at it.

As reality would have it, we don't live in an ideal world. If we did, mothers and fathers would be able to modify their work schedules to happily accommodate their families. In the meantime, which will probably be for a long time, the task at hand is to figure out what arrangement best suits each family's needs. The world has changed gradually and if you read enough magazines geared to working moms, you can become convinced that there are plenty of women out there making lots more money than their husbands. In truth, however, this remains the exception, not the rule. Much more often than not, when the couple's consensus is that more parental time is required at home, the financially expedient thing for the family dictates that Mom be the one to manage the home front and Dad be the one to keep earning his heftier paychecks.

This is a vicious cycle, but one likely to still be operative when my daughters are having their children. Until men begin having babies, most couples will find truly equitable parenting choices hard to come by. This doesn't have to be viewed as a terrible injustice. For one thing it is a temporary arrangement with innumerable permutations, and for another, delightful opportunities are available to homemakers that are not available to their partners who head out the door to work each day.

When I was pregnant with my third child, I spearheaded a fund-raiser for my children's school. Together with a steering committee of four other women, and despite the school director's reservations, I chaired the first large-scale fund-raiser the twenty-five-year-old school had ever undertaken. When I look back on the experience, I know that it was my first practical endeavor with public relations, business principles, public speaking, significant leadership, and team dynamics. Despite having to win over an apathetic parent body who put the extent of their disposable incomes toward their children's tuitions, we netted an excess of $35,000 on that one-night event. Ten years later, I still use the skills and insights I learned while working on that auction.

Just about any woman who has dedicated blocks of time to domesticity can tell similar stories. In commenting on her appointment as the first woman dean of Columbia Law School, Barbara Aronstein Black made the following remarks:

> The message is not merely that a woman was appointed dean at Columbia Law School, but a woman who did what I did: who took on the traditional duties and obligations and joys of the woman's role, who traveled a terribly circuitous path back to the job that she wanted, whose work was not the quantity that the more direct male path would have produced. What it suggests is that this kind of life experience is relevant to the professional world, perhaps even important, perhaps even critical. I really do believe that where I am today has everything to do with the years I spent hanging on to a career by my fingernails.

Any one of a thousand things can provide a woman a tip-off that she needs to take some time off or cut back on her work schedule. For me it was the fact that, after my fourth child was born, I began going through baby-sitters and nannies faster than disposable diapers. It didn't take me long to realize that with four kids under seven years of age, my home had been, at least temporarily, commandeered by chaos. It was a situation only a mother could love. So I put my plans to return to work on hold and cuddled up with sweatshirts and blue jeans, board books and bottles until some of the dust settled. The best I could do for my kids was the best any mother could do—take my cues from personal considerations, not someone else's ideology.

Think Sequentially, Then Be Ready for Anything

In my dictionary, sequence is defined as "a set of things that belong next to each other on some principle of order, a series without gaps." Much has been written about the virtues of walking the career-motherhood trail in a sequential fashion, taking one thing at a time in a reasonable order. Some of what I've said thus far in this book encourages such an approach: come of age before you get married; attend to your career aspirations before having kids; and take time off from work when you have children, but be prepared to go back. Over the short term, this is all well and good. The thing about motherhood and career over the long haul, however, is that a "principle of order" may be hard to discern.

Since having my first child, I've tried repeatedly to impose a sensible order on what I'm going to do next or to project a sequence on my career comings and goings. Invariably, though, just when I make a plan, something happens to change it. Attempting to achieve professional continuity has been a little like riding a Ferris wheel that is being loaded or unloaded, that stops and starts but never really gets going. When I got tired of trying to explain to people why I wasn't doing clinical work from time to time, I adopted that lovely term "sabbatical" to describe my intervals away from clinical medicine. If a man could take a sabbatical from professional life and go trekking in Tibet, why, I asked myself, couldn't I take a sabbatical for having a baby, raising worthwhile children, or even building a home? Trekking may be sexier or more self-actualizing (whatever that means), but my sabbaticals for motherhood are intended to both immediately and eventually make the world a better place to live.

Perhaps a more useful principle of order with which to direct time off from professional pursuits to be a mother, more useful anyway than the iffy and inflexible deadlines we've become accustomed to, would take its lead from what we hope to accomplish during these sabbaticals. Initially, for instance, I wanted to nurse my babies for their first year of life and wanted to spend enough time with them to give them a sense of security. With one child and a little creative scheduling, I was able to do this and still work full-time. With two, three, and four children, because my time at home was increasingly divvied up and my goals were always changing to accommodate growing kids, it became trickier to combine mothering with work away from home. Even so, the uneven nature of my professional comings and goings only appears uneven in the context of the straight lines that have always defined professional undertakings. From the standpoint of sensible child rearing, coming and going as kids' needs dictate makes perfect sense. The problem we have with reckoning home and work is that the two worlds are based on very different imperatives; the former is notoriously unpredictable while the latter demands almost slavish predictability.

Temporal sequencing, then, can frustrate the most dedicated and organized scheduler. Home is an apple and work is an orange, and trying to add them together leaves you with a curious sum. Still, many women are able to devise ways to make sense of this sum when they are backed by a partner who truly comprehends the dilemma, or when they are able to hire good help to fill the gaps. (A sequence, recall, doesn't have gaps.)

Because male partners who are willing to spend half their time as wives are hard to come by, an entire industry has grown up around procuring, training, and keeping nannies. Nanny newsletters targeted to employers and employees discuss the nitty-gritty of pay and time off as well as how to avoid hurt feelings. Videos demonstrate everything from how to interview a nanny to first-aid tips every baby-sitter should know. Agencies specialize in matching particular family needs with just the right nanny. These businesses have sprung up to address the fact that someone needs to care for children when parents are otherwise engaged.

This industry does not, however, include the sort of nannies-for-life like Mary Poppins, who floated through our premarital fantasies and helped fuel our myths about work and family. Poppins was a fictional product of the nonfictional British class system in which a whole social layer of individuals was dedicated to serving those of another layer. Being a classless society, in theory anyway, we don't produce many women willing to dedicate their adult lives to raising other people's children. Yet professional women often structure their expectations around the notion that seamless surrogate care abounds.

In our upwardly mobile society, home child care most often falls to young women who have yet to begin their own families or mature women who have empty nests. Either profile has its downside from the standpoint of continuous care. Young women go off and get better jobs, husbands, kids, or all of the above, and older women develop health problems or have relatives who eventually need their caregiving attention. Almost inevitably, the "sticky floor" phenomenon—found in homes wherever young children live, that keeps us from getting anywhere on time, awakens us numerous times during the night, ruins our favorite clothes, loses socks, spills lemonade on the new carpet, breaks dishes, makes babies fall asleep just as we're ready to carry them out the door, and derails our best-laid plans through all manner of other mischief—jumps up and snatches even the best nanny or baby-sitter at the worst possible moment.

My saga of sitters is not unusual. First came Mary, a white-haired retiree who magically soothed my colicky kid during her interview. She stayed for the first year, living out, until I began my internship and needed live-in help. Next I found Leslie, an energetic twenty-year-old, who I hired for her gentleness. She lived with us until I finished my first year of residency, then she left to go back to school and, a year later, have her own baby. A few months after Leslie left, my second child was born, and I hired Hafdis, a twenty-two-year-old Icelander who was here while her husband attended school. She stayed until her husband graduated four years later, then connected us with Hrefna, another Icelandic woman, who lived with us for six months. Hrefna left when her visa expired, about a month before my fourth child was born. I then went through a slew of sitters, none of whom, except for Candace, could quite abide the chaos in our home. But Candace didn't show up for work one day and sent a letter sometime later from another state, detailing the extent of her eating disorder and need for professional help. Eventually Laurel saved the day, hanging in here for several years until she too got married and had babies (she named one after my youngest). Heather overlapped Laurel and kept our lives sane for two or three more years until she graduated from college and went to Japan to teach English.

In the twilight of my need for sitters, Valerie worked for us off and on, but by then, because there was no longer a baby for a nanny to bond with, the bloom was off the baby-sitting business in our house. Besides which, let's face it, lots of jobs pay better and come with more predictable hours, not to mention a whole lot less bickering. Nannies and baby-sitters leave for the same reasons working moms need them; both sets of women need to make money and get a life. The difference, of course, is that what the nanny leaves is the mother's life.

Another development that confounds most nannies' long-term viability (one more development for which young mothers are grossly unprepared) is that as children get older the same surrogate care that made perfect sense when they were tiny becomes anachronistic. The lovable, huggable, wonderful woman who was great at getting spit stains out of little (but expensive) Swedish cotton play clothes and to whom your children ran when they wanted an "owie" kissed may not be the caretaker who can artfully mediate sibling disputes, inspire a child to greater reading heights, or go the distance with verbally demanding children. Again, this comes as a surprise to most women. Regardless of how many times this has been experienced, it's rarely talked about as something to expect.

A friend of mine landed the job of her dreams as an executive with a large entertainment corporation when her children were five and eight years old. She had always worked, and with this job she thought she had died and gone to heaven. The benefits and pay were so good that, despite the overtime and traveling demanded of her, she jumped in, full speed ahead. The same live-in nanny who had been with the family for several years continued her routine of getting the kids off to school, picking them up afterward, fixing dinner, and being Mom and Dad when both parents were traveling. About a year and a half into the job, my friend announced that she was thinking about quitting. "I have a wonderful husband, two fantastic kids, the job of my dreams, and good help," she confided to me one day. "I just can't figure out why I'm so profoundly unhappy."

As she contemplated her situation over the next several months, she realized that her children's lives had become very interesting, yet she was missing out on most of it. The time she did have at home seemed to be commandeered by the kids' demands; they increasingly wanted her validation in preference to the nanny's. When she finally did stop working for her dream employer, it came as a relief on many counts. The nanny moved out to care for her aging sister, and my friend became a full-time mom for the first time since her children were born. A woman of great talent and resourcefulness, she eventually became a freelance consultant with more control over the important aspects of her life.

She had initially, as most of us do, believed that as her children grew, so too would her ability and desire to work. She found what most working mothers with more than one child discover: The sequence we expect is rarely the one we get, and every good sequence needs gaps.

Swear by the "F" Word

Every mother with young children who has ever worked outside her home has a story to tell about patching solutions together to accommo-date the unexpected. Maybe some years down the scientific road, probably about the same time men are able to have babies, kids will be genetically engineered to be resistant to illness and injury. Until then, couples with kids will be using the wing-and-prayer technique to get to work each day.

This technique relies heavily on flexibility, which is hard to come by for anyone other than yourself in the working world. Here, two flexible jobs are better than one; if Mom has to be at a deposition, maybe Dad can cover her at home and vice versa. This arrangement also depends upon mutually respectful moms and dads. More often than not, though, the woman makes the last-minute phone calls to cancel commitments when a willful virus is having its way with Junior.

This situation arises with such regularity that some companies and geographic areas have opened sick-children centers. Because, in our cul-ture, the prevailing credo is "hallowed be productivity," anything that hin-ders getting the job done—even sick kids—is just a nuisance to be brain-stormed into the background. Despite having made adjustments when faced with a sick kid that, in retrospect, were not always brilliant from a parenting perspective, I can say that I never got desperate enough to leave one of my children in a sick-child repository. When my children are turning to their therapists in the year 2010 with stories about their upbringing, I want them to counterbalance some of their complaints with the redemptive knowledge that at least they got to be sick at home. Most of the time anyway.

I wouldn't have wanted my kids to think they were abnormal, so on the learning curve end of my parenting career, which will probably go on until I die, I was known to take a recuperating child along to a clinic set-ting. A recuperating child is one who has been sick for days or has been vomiting all night and who climbs out of bed in the morning looking the positive picture of health. Experience tells you that if you send this child to school, she will crumple within an hour or two, and a phone call from the school office will fetch you from your denial. If, on the other hand, you keep her home just to be safe, she will dance circles around you all day.

At any rate, on just such a day, I was doing the just-to-be-safe thing with one of my daughters who had already kept me home for two days but who looked good enough that morning to accompany me to the office. I was just finishing up a wound repair, when my three-year-old pushed open the door and wandered in as though the minor surgery suite was the snack room at school. Just as I would in any situation that wasn't supposed to happen the way it was happening, I contemplated my options. I could pretend that this was the Big Happy Family Medical Clinic and introduce my daughter to the patient as though this sort of intrusion was to be expected. Symbolic of the bind in which mothers find themselves too often and not unlike bringing your dog to a company picnic, this option could have one of several outcomes: the patient would be delighted, indifferent, or offended.

Hedging my bets against the possibility that the patient in question was of the latter persuasion, I considered claiming that my three-year-old was a patient that had escaped from another room and then calling for help. I also thought about crediting her presence to the receptionist and requesting her retrieval at once. Fortunately, as I said, I had just finished suturing and was able to snap off my gloves before she got too far into the room. Whether a wing or a prayer came through for me that time I'll never know.

What I do know, however, is that it is a miserable, no-win, rock-and-hard-place prospect to face a day with a full schedule only to find that a child has a fever, rash, earache, or tummy ache and can't go to school as planned that day, or that the nanny is having car, boyfriend, or motivational troubles and is either running late or has called in sick. What goes through my mind at times like these is nothing original, nothing that hasn't been contemplated millions of times by other frustrated moms.

Let's see. She doesn't look that bad. Maybe I could send her to school and no one would notice the double stream of green snot billowing from her nostrils. No, that won't do. Maybe if I cancel my patients at the last minute, they will be understanding and not think of me forever after as unreliable just because this is the third time this month I've had to do this. Hmm, too risky. Maybe if I call my husband, he'll come directly home and take a turn at this medic business. But that would be an unlikely first. I know, I'll call every sitter on my crossed out, erased, rewritten, outdated, and generally exhausted list of backup baby-sitting personnel. I'll say, "Hi, it's me. Can you sit right now? . . . Yeah, right now. . . . Oh, until about five o'clock this evening. . . . Oh, you have a life? . . . Oh, okay. Well then, maybe next time."

In order to maintain their sense of dignity, if not sanity, working mothers go in one of several directions. Many develop—or at least pretend to develop—thick skins toward their employers, clients, fellow workers, and nannies, but hopefully not toward their kids. In doing so they put everyone on notice that things may not be as predictable as they ("they," everyone and "they," the women) would like, but that one way or another business will get taken care of. That's it; no apologies. In doing this, however, the old adage about how women have to be twice as good at what they do to be considered half as good is brought into play. The mother who takes this hard-line approach has to make herself worth waiting for, which is admirable but also another time- and energy-consuming process.

Some women just keep on keeping on and never come up for air long enough to become premeditated about how to do things better. They hobble through life's unpredicted frustrations, apologizing as they go and always hoping for the best. With one child, this can work. With more than one, the time of torment can be prolonged by years. Even for the most happy-go-lucky among us, this is a demoralizing position to be in.

Others take the career bull by its horns and construct ways of doing business that revolve around their home lives, rather than the other way around. This approach inevitably lends the greatest flexibility to a woman with children. Being able to work very early, during naps, late at night, in your old maternity clothes, and at your own pace lends itself nicely to accommodating children. It is not, however, something that may be immediately possible and may take years to put realistically (read, gainfully) in place.

Still, inventing flexibility can lead to very satisfying ways of doing business—even after children have left the nest. While in a deli buying lunch one day recently, I ran into the professor who taught me organic chemistry in college. During my days in her classroom, she had a reputation for being the most beautiful, brilliant, engaging, and well-put-together professor on campus. Many of the male professors, in fact, envied her style, charm, popularity with the students, and teaching success. Rare is the prof who can make organic chemistry not just palatable but delicious.

On the day we were ordering our turkey sandwiches, however, my mentor looked almost frumpy. "Oh," she said chuckling her musical laugh in response to my greeting. "I was hoping I wouldn't see anyone I knew. I'm writing an organic chemistry textbook and often don't even get dressed on Tuesdays and Thursdays." To put her at ease, I told her about another friend of mine, mother of three, who has decided that her goal in life is to make as much money as she can while in her pajamas. The professor's eyes brightened at that thought. "That's it," she said. "Sounds good to me."

Of course the pajama part of this fantasy is just symbolic of the discrepancy that exists between being dressed for career success and being dressed for success with kids. Children demand flexibility of everything, not just time but wardrobe too. When my children were very little and I was leaving them with a nanny, I'd say good-bye first and then head to my room to dress for the day at the office. Rather than venturing back into the main part of the house for another round of kisses and hugs and running the risk of getting spit, dripped, spilled, or thrown up on after getting ready for work, I'd duck out the back door to my car. To this day I am reluctant to pick up my kids from school if I'm dressed for anything other than, well, being with the kids. Wrestling bicycles into the back of a sport-utility vehicle is rough on panty hose, and silk has a hard time with eager sweaty hugs.

Nonetheless, wardrobe considerations are an itsy-bitsy dimension to flexibility. The most important aspect is thinking about the demands of home and career in a way that allows for change. Doing things one way for a time, then adapting as circumstances demand, is a lovely way to thrive through the child-rearing years, a way to maximize your chances of landing on your feet. If women and men—both and together—would enter the state of parenthood expecting a multifaceted process of discovery and not a predictable checklist of entitlements, everyone would make happier headway. To be able to say, "Let's figure out what this situation requires," rather than, "This shouldn't be happening to me," is to create the best of all possible worlds for yourself, your kids, your spouse, and your career.

Hang on by Your Fingernails

Being cut loose from a schedule that revolves around the working world can be unnerving for someone who has always worked. Rather than heeling to the dictates of an early-morning business meeting, first patient, deposition, or power breakfast, you may find yourself wandering around in your pajamas at noon. Nap schedules and feedings conduct the remainder of the day, and little things—like taking a shower, getting some exercise, or going to the grocery store—loom large. I can remember when just getting my legs shaved was quite an accomplishment.

With this other world as a backdrop, the things that once made you jump from bed in the morning or go looking for everything you could find on a subject begin to slip into oblivion. New subjects, ones you never dreamed would command your passions, take precedence. Where once you could rattle off the companies comprising the Dow Jones Industrial Average and what they were trading for on any given day, you now have at your fingertips the brand names and prices of all available breast pumps. The details of cases you argued most convincingly before juries have lost their relevance; the details of child development now occupy that corner of your cerebral cortex. The stack of books you kept next to your bed are no longer the latest novels; they've been replaced by parenting tomes you are too tired to read in bed anyway. For this you went to graduate school!

Some women, it's true, can't stand this existence. Others not only get accustomed to it, but come to dread the working world and the specter of returning to it. The problem with not working is the same as with working too much; most of us get used to anything pretty quickly and cease to be able to see what we're missing. It's like the clutter that accumulates in a household over time and becomes an expected part of the scenery after a while.

A good friend of mine from medical school worked straight through three children over eight years. When her youngest was three, Angela, her nanny of ten years, quit to begin her own family. My friend, unable after many tries to find as reliable a replacement, cut back her office hours to coincide with her children's school schedules. She called me one day and confessed, "I never knew how good I had it with Angela all those years, but I also never knew how much of the kids' lives I was missing." Staying at home can have the same effect in reverse. You forget what you are missing by not working.

Full- or part-time mothering can often be a catalyst for changing a woman's professional direction. Given the new perspective of more home time and less outside work, many women begin to see work options they never before considered. When I stopped working after my fourth was born (it was only going to be for a few months but stretched into years), I had a hard time not being a doctor at all. I had spent too many years thinking of myself as a doctor, besides which my husband never thought of me as anything else. Clinical medicine, however, was not the great fit with family life I had talked myself into believing it would be. No matter how I tried to abbreviate my hours, somehow it was difficult to get away from work's demands.

I began to focus on the many things other than clinical medicine for which people use medical degrees. Many a medical researcher, administrator, or writer, I found, also took advantage of an M.D. Because I could keep my professional identity and have the flexibility I needed to accommodate my wild and woolly brood, I began writing a child-health column for a big-city newspaper and sold reprints to several parenting magazines. The pay left something to be desired, but so did that of full-time mothering. Having to say something thorough, informative, and enlightening on a medical topic each week forced me to stay on top of at least one area of medicine. When I returned to clinical medicine, I continued to write my column because it remained a mix of mom and medicine that appealed to me more than the hands-on world.

It is no wonder, really, that women are now cited as the largest group of entrepreneurs. A whole generation of women came of age expecting to be able to do whatever they wanted. It makes perfect sense that when these women found the traditional path didn't take them where they needed to go, they regrouped and charted new territory in their fields. Sometimes the necessity of being home, free from having to think about immediate work-related problems, can inform whole new ways of thinking about lives and livelihoods.

For a variety of reasons, women who decide to remain at home for any significant length of time would do well to keep abreast of developments in their professional field. Even though most professional women don't stop working with the intent of never going back to it, time has a way of reconfiguring expectations with more children, household projects, and family emergencies. At first, some arbitrary return time frames most maternity leaves, regardless of how lengthy. When the children are weaned or in preschool or in kindergarten, that's when Mom will go back to being her working self again. Yet things rarely become any easier; life just doesn't happen that way.

What does happen is that children grow up and eventually leave home, and that old professional focus or a new one that grew out of it begins to look better than ever in the void children leave in their wake.

Make Yourself at Home

Someone should do an entire book of home-office stories if it hasn't already been done. Working at home is not only a wonderful opportunity to get a grip on two worlds at once, but provides much needed comic relief from the often stressful nature of keeping many balls in the air at one time.

Of course, women have been working at home from time immemorial, sewing, cooking, taking in laundry, doing clerical work, bookkeeping, or performing just about any task that can be done in the absence of a full-fledged factory. Still, the presence of a home income-generating endeavor took on an official gleam with the arrival of computers, fax machines, and copiers. Somehow a sewing machine in the living room that earned several hundred dollars a month didn't emanate quite the machismo that office equipment in the spare bedroom does, even when the latter isn't as lucrative as the former. Yet that sewing machine set the stage for the concept that work could be where the home is.

Having been trying to get things done with children underfoot for eons, women are particularly well-suited to taking the concept of working at home as many steps further as it can go. What's so different, after all, about looking for the kitchen shears only to find that the kids have them out in the tree house, and trying to print out a report only to find the kids have taken all the paper out of your printer to make paper airplanes. Life is truly a beach where kids are concerned, and the house—and home office—is a series of tide pools just waiting to be picked over.

Setting up shop at home, then, is one way to bridge the chasm between family priorities and money-making necessities. When the home business requires interacting with the public, however, be it in person or by phone, things can get a bit trickier. Kids are not intimidated by the glitz of office machines, but rather, tend to bring everything down to their own level. Highfalutin wheeling and dealing is just one more no-no opportunity for children.

I know this all too well. Several years ago, I had been corresponding with an editor at a large metropolitan newspaper in the East about writing a regular column for the paper. After many discussions, we were about ready to go ahead with the idea, and I was just waiting to hear the final decision. With four kids under the age of nine and a part-time office practice, however, I was hardly sitting by the phone waiting for a reply.

One evening about 6:00 P.M. California time, just as I was feeding the kids dinner, the phone rang. On this particular night, because my husband and I were heading to a friend's birthday party for dinner, the *cuisine des enfants* consisted of takeout from McDonald's. I was busily arranging happy meals on plastic dishes, avoiding the kids' greedy grabs, when the phone interrupted my progress. Against my better judgment and with hungry kids flailing for food, I grabbed the receiver thinking to make quick work of the call. Folding my head sideways over the receiver, I kept at my task, issuing a housewifely hello. If my guard was ever up, it went down at 5:30 P.M. my time, since both coasts were usually out of the office by then.

Of course, it was an editor from the paper calling to congratulate me on the news that they would be launching my column the following month. "I'm so pleased," I said, hardly stopping to wonder why this editor was still in the office at 9:00 P.M. her time (now there was a woman who needed a home office). My kids, meanwhile, heard the unmistakable change in my tone as I slipped into my official business voice. I should have kept to the housewifely pitch; children are programmed to be on their worst behavior whenever a parent is on the phone, but when that parent has adopted her business telephone voice, even worst behavior has another level of depravity.

On this particular occasion, my six-year-old daughter, accidentally or on purpose depending on whom you asked, squeezed ketchup onto my four-year-old son's shirt. My son then transmogrified into a small but deadly hurricane of fists, kicks, and screams. He managed to retaliate with twice as much ketchup, causing an altercation that would have done light-weight boxing proud. At that point, my youngest and oldest joined the ketchup caper just because it looked like fun.

I did the only thing I could, being hardwired as I was to the phone in the family room and therefore unable to move away from the chaos. Except for uttering, "Okay, sweetie, just a minute," once or twice gently, I pretended nothing out of the ordinary was happening. Somehow the newspaper deal was clinched despite an all-out ketchup fight in progress on all sides of me. I suppose all's well that end's well; the column, it turned out, had even more staying power than the ketchup stains on the family room carpet.

And I learn from each episode. To avoid home business quandaries of the ketchup-flinging sort, I now go for my cordless headset when answer-ing the phone. This gizmo is the wonder of wiring wizardry I treasure most among my electronic armamentarium. This simple modification on the decades-old cordless phone allows me to morph at will from mom to doc to writer to friend to soccer coach without missing a beat or getting a crook in my neck, and with both hands at the ready for everything else that needs attention while I'm on the phone. It may sound sick, a bit over the top, to wander the house looking like a switchboard operator from the fifties, my family never knowing whether I'm on or off the phone and occasionally asking, "Are you talking to me, Mom?" But what a wan-dering headset lacks in personal interactive aesthetics, it makes up for in efficiency. And with several irons in the home fire at one time, there's much to be said for efficiency.

Despite being a business machine junkie, however, even I have my limits. I will never own a video phone. Woe to me if casual callers could be privy to what is really going on behind my calm exterior voice. I've done long-distance deals with a two-year-old hanging on my leg wailing;

I've sat with my hair wrapped in a towel at 5:30 in the morning talking business to New York; I've done telephone interviews while mixing stir fry or folding laundry; I've hopped directly from the shower to the phone and had no one be the wiser. No, a video phone would never do.

Still, being able to work at home has been a blessing I wouldn't trade for all the kitchen equipment in the tree house. I worship at the altar of all the business machines and technology that make it possible for me to be home when the guy comes to fix the dishwasher at 9:00 in the morning, to be home when the school calls to say my eight-year-old is sick, to be home when the dog gets out of the yard at noon, to be home when my fifteen-year-old calls to ask if I'll transport the swim team to practice at 1:30, and to be home when the kids want to have friends over after school. Being able to complete my medical charts, make callbacks from a home desk, and take a weekend call from the sidelines of a soccer game are welcome products of current technology and attitude. When career and family both command attention, working at home gives new meaning to the saying "Home is where the heart is."

Workaholic Beware

Despite the sweet flexibility it provides, working at home can be dangerously seductive. The line separating home from office is much more difficult to discern when the distance to your desk is traveled down a hallway at home rather than through a subway tunnel or crosstown traffic. The temptation for people who love their work, who are ambitious by nature, or who find work a path of less resistance than the one leading toward kids is to heed the call of the work space at the expense of time with their families. When you don't remove yourself from the premises or dress for work, it's easy to work all the time.

For years (decades, centuries), workaholism was predominantly a male phenomenon. Now that women have established themselves in the work world, workaholism is becoming pandemic. Bringing in a hefty paycheck and commanding the respect of your peers is heady stuff that doesn't come without work and more work. When that work is done at home, it is harder to put work aside than it would be in conventional digs. When placed in a domestic setting day in and day out, work does what children and housework have always done and beckons continuously. That "woman's work is never done" just becomes more inclusive when considering gainful employment from a home base.

When a home office is the backdrop, work's pervasiveness is only one of the problems that can develop. Those who take cultural notes on how society's behavior changes from decade to decade have observed that while home has begun to harbor our work, our work has begun to harbor us from home. This, too, has been men's realm for many years. As families' needs for dual incomes steadily increases domestic stress, however, both income earners may find solace in their work from the chaos of being married or divorced with children. When work, either some or all of it, takes place at home, that satellite office looks awfully good when things heat up in the kitchen or bedroom. The tendency to gravitate from the family's disorderly arena to work's orderly arena, while only natural, can create more conflict than it avoids. Someone is bound to be left feeling "stuck" with the kids.

Women, nonetheless, are wonderfully notorious for putting children first and work second. Despite this talent, a balance has to be struck between technology that makes homes more convenient and that which insidiously deprives children of the unfettered attention they deserve. The computer makes writing, artwork, investing, research, and communication swifter; it also changes these things into rewarding pastimes that are hard to put aside. Fax machines have made the postal and even overnight mail service lag times obsolete; they also ring at all hours of the day and night, begging to be answered. Laptop computers that make work portable can make it too portable. And cellular phones have made parents more secure in the time they spend away from kids; but these phones don't provide the same security to children who are left alone—even with a cell-phone number at the ready.

After three decades of traveling to offices, women are making changes in the traditional (some say male) model of work in the workplace. They are demanding and getting flex time and part-time schedules and family-leave time. The danger in going to the next level of time management by bringing their work home, however, is that the traditional model will trail them right into their family rooms. Perhaps the diciest aspect of working at home is that there is no distance from the distraction. The psycholog-ical component to being at work has no way of being interrupted—well, maybe a ketchup fight would do it—unless you have the mental discipline to draw certain lines.

Keeping the raison d'être of the home office foremost in your mind is a good way to keep those lines drawn. The goal, after all, is to be more available to your family, not less. And not just in body, but in mind.

Remember the Old Woman Who Lived in a Shoe

It doesn't take much when you are trying to straddle two universes to have so many children you don't know what to do. Giving them broth without bread, spanking them soundly, and putting them to bed is not an option unless you want a social worker or the police knocking on your door. The first thing I do when reading a story about a very successful woman is skim to the part about kids. Any? How many? How old? This perverse curios-ity consumes me because I know how much of my attention during prime career-development time has been focused on my children. I also recog-nize the price I've paid in career dollars and standing to get my kids up and running the best way I know how.

How to proceed simultaneously with children and career, however, hasn't always been obvious, perhaps because the parameters, just like the kids, keep changing. I carry on a never-ending conversation with my hus-band about the trade-offs. Should I work more so we can afford the extras that enhance the quality of family life, or is it more important to be tightly budgeted but available? Does it matter if we eat take-out several nights a week so I can toe the professional line, or does home cooking with its nutritional benefits and opportunities for family interaction outweigh some of my career inclinations? Should I hire someone to drive the kids around after school so I can work longer hours, or will I be missing out on all the best moments for finding out what's going on in their lives? Inevitably, there are no correct answers to these questions, only my ongoing effort to strike a balance that is mutually fortunate for my family and myself. No one else can make these decisions because no one else lives with a set of circumstances identical to mine.

Several themes emerge from profiles of successful working mothers. Those who have achieved and maintained status in rigid careers that provide little flexibility almost always have very supportive and flexibly employed partners. Role reversal is more common among high-powered women with children, with the husband not only following his wife where her jobs lead, but also supplying a good deal of the kid care and other domestic management.

Another trend sees women stepping quickly up to their career plates when their children are very young, developing respectable batting averages, then retreating to some extent as their kids enter elementary school. This is exactly what you wouldn't expect, given the prospective inclination to stay home with children when they are very young and then return to work when they enter school. The dearth of women in high places in the scientific, corporate, and political worlds, however, has more to do with the tendency of children and careers to become demanding simultaneously than it does with any male-directed intent to keep women down. The woman who has her children as she is working her way up the corporate ladder may find that she is promoted to the executive position of her dreams just when her kids develop an interest in sports, performing arts, or music. Now she is not just missing the kids' naps, meals, or bedtimes, but the focal points of their existences: the swim meets, soccer games, plays, and concerts.

A friend of mine had bided her time in an academic setting for years while her daughter was in preschool. When her daughter was in second grade, my friend was awarded a five-year term as department chair, one of her career goals. She kept the position for just two years before resigning. "Not only was I bringing work home every night," she said when I asked her about this decision, "but, more importantly, I looked ahead and realized I would have had to miss every softball game during the coming year." This dilemma, this tendency of careers to rev up just as children's schedules take off, is the essence of the sticky floor. Rather than planning for this, most women are ambushed by it.

This is why another frequent common denominator for successful women is that they don't, for the most part, have large families. This stands to reason; every child makes decisions more complicated. A woman with one child and a very involved partner can often comfortably time-share the kid end of things. With two children, scheduling logistics are double the trouble. Three will always push the dual-income parenting envelope, and four can forcibly rein in a brilliant career. There is no temporal economy of scale when it comes to additional children. You can shop for bargains and buy in bulk, but you can't make two class plays or parent conferences into one—unless, of course, we're talking twins. Even twins, though, will eventually pull your attention in different directions.

There is also, family-sized packages notwithstanding, very little monetary economy of scale. The family that heads down the private school road with their first child, for example, may have difficult decisions to make about whether to continue as their brood increases in number. Childcare costs, tuitions, summer camp fees, medical insurance premiums, food bills, dental work, housing costs, and the price of incidentals will go up markedly every time you add a member to your family. You can tuck the second or third kid in a basket in your closet and call it the nursery for a few months, but sooner or later that baby is going to need more space and always more of your time.

The pulls between time and money are in diametrically opposing directions. The imperative to support a burgeoning budget—my husband calls ours a two-thousand-pound gorilla—beckons a woman toward money-making pursuits. The attention requirements of an additional child beckons her away from money-making pursuits. And while we make at least some rudimentary educational effort to instruct children about financial planning, similar efforts regarding family size and dynamics would be eaten up and spit out by educational planning politics. As a result, from early on, children solve math problems involving pennies, oranges, or miles, but never dwell on the dicier topics of numbers of children. An effort of the latter sort wouldn't have to take aim at parents who want more than one or two children—some parents are just the ones to have more—but only at how the numbers play out. What if all those oranges cost not pennies, but thousands of dollars each year? How many would Johnny and Janey be able to afford?

Predicting the future is an endeavor fraught with error, dashed hopes, and frustration. Preparing for and anticipating the future's likelihoods, however, is a necessary and fundamental component of parenting. So very much of what it takes to raise competent children is right in front of our eyes from the very beginning. What remains is that those of us who choose to have children understand that this choice has its price—our time, our money, our emotional commitment, our future. Broth, bread, and old shoes won't cover it all.

Chapter Four

Fathers Are Different from Mothers

The basic discovery about any people is the discovery of the relationship between men and women.

—Pearl S. Buck

Mothers who embraced feminism and envisioned their lives on a par with their husbands made the enormous assumption that all the work of making money and raising a family would be shared equally. There have, it turns out, been several problems with putting this supposition into practice: men didn't make the same assumption; men and women are fundamentally different in many ways; and it takes generations to change culturally established roles. Understanding how the theory of equality differs from the reality can help prevent disappointment and frustration, but bringing the two closer together will depend on how the fathers and mothers of the future are being raised now.

Synchronize Your Parenting Watches

If I had to illustrate the way my time gets used, the picture would look like one of those pot holders woven from loops that every kid makes. The net effect is bumpy, the color scheme random, and the end result never quite big enough for the purpose. What it has going for it is a utilitarian nature and an ability to accommodate small pleasures.

My husband's picture, I'm quite sure about this, would look very different. He might draw a day planner or show you his office appointment schedule—in any case it would be an evenly lined portrait of time. It would not include things like wrapping a birthday present, packing a child's bag for an overnight, braiding a daughter's hair, or starting the dishwasher at the last minute. It wouldn't include these because he doesn't use time this way, but rather paces or sits in the idling car wondering what could be taking me so long. Most fathers and mothers approach time use very differently. If it is ever understood why so many more men play so much more golf than women, the essence of this gender time gap might be understood.

Men tend to operate in a business mode, wherein everything gets pushed aside to make time for singular considerations. Because this modus operandi facilitates thoroughness and gets the job done, it is admired and rewarded in the work world. Once the job is done, men are also good at pushing everything aside to relax—say for eighteen holes or so.

Mothers rarely have the luxury to compartmentalize their time this way. Most moms these days have to push things aside to accomplish necessary work, just like the men in their lives. The big difference between the mom and the dad, however, is that after getting the job done, the mom faces, not five hours on the golf course, but five hours of another category of work. The old saying "Man may work from sun to sun, but woman's work is never done" isn't as old-fashioned as it sounds.

The gender time gap inevitably begets marital tensions. The man thinks he is done for the day; the woman has a list of chores that need to be done. The woman finally sits down to steal a few precious minutes to read after being on her feet all day at work and then at home, and the man wants to talk finances. The man sees the weekend as his time; the woman sees the weekend as family time. The woman drops into bed exhausted; the man, who has been lying in bed reading for a while, wants amore.

The gap that develops between a father's and mother's ability to attend to their careers is more significant, however, than the uneven juxtaposition of their personal time. Beyond an innate drive and ambition, time is the key element that allows someone to go the extra distance necessary to become a standout in his or her field. The ubiquity of stray moments and unruly hours on the maternal side of the gender time gap confounds mothers in their career ascents with great regularity.

More often than not, it is the dad, not the mom, who calls home to say, "I'll be working late so don't hold dinner," but the mom, not the dad, who stays home when a child wakes up with a fever. More often than not, it is Dad whose job takes a family to a new location and Mom who turns down the promotion that would require her to travel regularly. More often than not, it is the father—assured that the family is in good hands—who has the freedom to jump through sequential career hoops, while the mother stands fairly still on her career time line. The so-called mommy track is more like an hour glass with sand running out than a track to any career destination.

And so it goes. When left to supervise their own young children, men often refer to it as baby-sitting; women never "baby-sit" for their own kids. An hour in this position feels like an eternity to many dads; to their spouses an hour with the kids is a momentary blur. And perhaps because time weighs more heavily in its structured manifestations, men often feel the need for vacations more keenly and regularly than do their wives.

Even vacations, times intended for relaxation, recreation, and rejuvenation, are experienced differently by mothers and fathers. What is a distinct break in routine and "free" time for Dad, is just more daily drudgery but with a change of scenery from Mom's perspective. Dad may return to work a week later, relaxed and ready to go. Mom on the other hand feels like she really needs a vacation once the family trip is over. Dad goes off to work with a clean slate; Mom faces her return to work amidst suitcases full of dirty laundry.

Reconciling this time gap will eventually do more to neutralize other aspects of the gender gap—at work, at home, at play—than any ten laws directed at creating equality between men and women. This reconciliation began during the "Me" era of the seventies when adults of every stripe were devolving into so many adolescents by saying, "What about me?" What scant good came out of so much navel contemplation lay in women's ability to finally view their time as something beyond a predestined role to serve husbands and children. Yet men and women both went too far toward serving themselves rather than their families. It would have been infinitely more useful had men adopted certain aspects of women's time perception while women were studying how to be like men. This would at least have served to narrow the gender time gap. And while part of this gap and some of the differences between men's and women's use of time may be irreconcilable, it wouldn't hurt for wives and husbands, mothers and fathers, parents and breadwinners to begin a cultural endeavor that would involve synchronizing their collective watches a little more closely.

Tell It Like It Is

A physician and mother of two young children was explaining how she manages to take calls for her busy primary-care group for a week at a time. "I'm essentially gone for an entire week every two months," she said. "I might as well be out of town so my husband has to step in and help out in a big way. He knows in advance, so he makes sure his office schedule is light, and really, he and the kids enjoy the time together." She laughed lightly and added, "Of course, at the end of the week the house is a disaster zone, and it takes me another whole week just to get the socks out of the bread box. But it works out pretty well."

This is a saga that resonates with many gainfully employed women. Husband and wife both work and when the wife is in charge of the home, everything gets done. When the husband steps up to the home plate, however, lots of things—especially housekeeping sorts of things—don't get done. A tacit and admittedly sometimes inadvertent line appears in the sandbox about which home agenda items are worthy of the father's time and attention, and which are not.

This is not to say that plenty of couples haven't worked out the kinks in the domestic time-share a family demands. They are, nonetheless, in a distinct minority, and an uneven truce often fills the space where equality might lie, as the story above illustrates. We are, sociologists tell us, making headway in this area, with men increasingly taking up the home reins so their wives can work or play. I've often wondered exactly what questions are asked to elicit this information. Does a questionnaire say, "Circle the appropriate answer regarding how much of the housecleaning you do each week: 10 percent, 50 percent, 90 percent, or none," or do these forms ask about specifics?

If I were designing a form I would go for the telltale information. "How many times," I would want to know of men filling in the data, "have you shopped for, prepared, delivered, and doled out soccer snacks, including the sliced oranges?" Partial answers wouldn't count because anybody can take directions. When a woman says, "Honey, I'll run to the store and get the snacks and cut up the oranges and put paper towels or baby wipes in the bag and also remember an extra plastic bag for the garbage if you will take the snacks to the game," a dad wouldn't be eligible to check the "soccer snacks" box on my questionnaire.

Or how about, "How many times have you done head lice detail?" I suppose some dads would consider having empathized with their wives and shuddering at appropriate intervals as having actually dirtied their hands, but not in my study. In order to even answer "Once," you have to have left whatever you were doing to go get the kid from school in the middle of the day; gone to the doctor or pharmacist to procure the treatment; washed the hair, combed out the nits, changed the bedding, vacuumed or wiped down the car upholstery, bagged the stuffed animals; reexamined every kid's hair daily for a week; and probably repeated all this several times. At least.

Volunteer time is another good category for determining who does what. "How many hours of volunteer time do you spend at your child's school each semester?" would be on my poll. Sorry, no points for attending back-to-school night, parent-teacher conferences, the class's fall camp out, the holiday potluck (not even for preparing the dish), the spring sing, or your kid's graduation. No points either for taking a few extra minutes at drop off to look through your child's work or classroom. By volunteer, I'm talking things like helping build the new play structure on Saturday morning, being the auctioneer at the fund-raiser, manning the watermelon booth during the jog-a-thon, serving on the board of directors or PTA, or doing the oh-so-rewarding lunch duty.

Lots of fathers earn points in areas that hold some independent interest for them, primarily sports. So, okay, dads can get points on my questionnaire for coaching, refereeing, or umpiring, for timing at swim meets, grooming the baseball fields, or announcing at events. And they get bonus points for preparing the food item required (in addition to time on the work grid) from their family for the bake sale or the snack bar that benefits the team. Bonus points are also available for signing up for one of those three-hour stints in the soda booth or concession stand. I know, I know. The guys would rather be watching the game. Funny thing, though; so would I.

I could go on. I haven't even mentioned how making costumes for the children's theater production counts, or how many points accrue to those who fix a meal, not because the spirit moves them, but because it's dinnertime and their wife is running late and everyone is hungry. And there are lots of points for thoroughly cleaning out a child's room (finding the other Barbie shoe; extracting and sorting the jumble from under the bed; knowing where to put the Lego, Brio, and puzzle pieces; and what to do with the plastic Sesame Street figures, collectable erasers, and omnipresent baseball cards). And yes, it counts even more if you can enlist the kid to help with the job and not get impatient in the process. Then when the room is clean, the dresser will need to be gone through to remove those clothes that haven't fit your child for the past year.

The 1997 figures from the Board of Labor Statistics tell the story of who does what at home as well as any questionnaire: the wage gap between men and women widened that year for the first time in nearly twenty years. In 1979 women's median earnings were 62 percent of men's. This number was then nudged all the way to 77 percent in 1993 before it began to slip to 75 percent, where it stood in 1997. Experts analyzing these numbers wondered why this dip would show up decades into the wage-earning trends begun by feminism and in the midst of a booming economy.

Two things might explain this phenomenon: reality and the learning curve. Women in my age cohort had tried on the gainfully employed mother role for years, running an uneasy slalom around workplace expectations and family demands. What we experienced didn't feel terribly liberated in many instances. We found that while feminism had, in a very brief time, given women the remarkable gift of being able to open almost any career door they chose, there was more to it than that. Twenty years after college, graduate school, or marriage, the ramifications of what happens when a huge segment of the population dramatically changes its culturally established roles with very little compensatory change from the rest of the population were beginning to become really obvious. It took that long to measure and begin to react to the fallout from a blithely—or at least naively—undertaken demographic shift.

It shouldn't come as a surprise that the reversal of the income gap occurred during a time of national economic well-being. The economic prosperity of the 1980s was built on the backs of women willing to take on two jobs: mother and wage earner. The recession that marked the late eighties and early nineties tightened the screws, making it difficult for women to step back from their jobs. It may well be that the return of economic prosperity allowed women to realign their energies toward their waiting families. Had a significant number of men taken this opportunity to address the work-family dilemma by assuming the domestic end of things, the wage gap might look better for women.

This didn't happen, however, and because the wage gap takes its cues from entrenched roles, it probably won't in my children's lifetimes. As long as women are the ones having the babies, they will continue to be more likely than men to trade gainful hours for time at home. As goes the resulting wage gap, so goes the likelihood that, even in the absence of babies, women are the ones most apt to cut back on paid hours when more time is needed at home. The substantial progress made in narrowing the wage gap is testimony to women's aspirations and ambitions, but these can stretch only so far. To further narrow the wage gap, men will have to come more fully into the domestic sphere, not only willingly, but comfortably.

Soccer snacks, anyone?

Make No Mistake, Sex Is Everything

There's an old but well-known episode of *Seinfeld* in which all the leading characters make a bet about who can go the longest without sex or masturbation. While trying to win the bet they all get irritable, irrational, or desperate, presumably for want of an orgasm. I'm a *Seinfeld* fan and laughed at the gags and underlying premise of the episode. I also, however, couldn't escape the feeling that the premarital population hasn't gained any insights during the past thirty years into the way women's sexual agendas differ from men's. There was Elaine, doing the same thing all my college and twenty-something female friends did before we were married—equating her sexual needs, timetable, and symptoms with those of the guys. Call this what you will—machisma, wishful thinking, disingenuousness, eagerness to please—but it often leads to a mutual misunderstanding between partners once the honeymoon is over. I call this *Seinfeld* phase of sexual experience "courtship sex."

In any event, men are apt to develop different expectations during courtship than women. Men are at least as and usually more interested in sex for the physical release it provides than they are for emotional intimacy, while the reverse tends to be true for women. And just as women's lives and bodies follow an up-and-down course through career, marriage, and motherhood, so too do their sexual interests. Men, as in life and career, generally follow a more even and predictable path where libido is concerned.

The symptoms of this have been the topic of TV talk shows, magazine coverage, humor, talk radio, medical inquiry, academic studies, and just about any other means of exploring a topic you can think of. The basis for my comments stems not from studies or other objectified modes of observation, but from the hundreds of conversations I've had about this with other women, primarily mothers. "It boils down to this," a marital therapist friend once commented. "The root of most problems that arise within a marriage has to do with the fact that women want more talk and collaboration, and men just want more sex." It's the oxymoron of our times that so much attention is riveted on romantic sex, while the disconnect between courtship sex and marital sex is rarely discussed openly. No wonder it comes as a surprise to both parties.

Many experts on marital relationships maintain that sex within a marriage is similar to temperament, that it has to do with how well matched a couple is in this particular regard. That's not what I hear. What looks like a well-matched couple may have as much to do with each partner's ability to tolerate and weather either a fundamental mismatch or periods of sexual incompatibility and still remain civil as it does with any ongoing cosmic symmetry of libidos. Such appearances may also relate to a woman's willingness to accommodate her partner's needs. Moreover, a good match can go bad under a variety of conditions, as when hormonal, psychological, or physical profiles change. For women, the most notable examples of such change include pregnancy, postpartum intervals, and menopause. Chronologically, it is the first two of these that frequently change a couple's sexual dynamics.

As discussed earlier in this book, a woman's overall focus is compellingly and dramatically redirected when she becomes a mother. Her ability to respond to her husband is modified at a time when he may be feeling most needy of her attention. Even routine interactions can begin to feel a little like negotiating a minefield. He says, "C'mere and tell me about your day," but means, "Let's have sex." She says, "I'm exhausted," and means, "I'm exhausted and that baby may wake up any minute so I sure hope you're not interested in sex." She says, "How was your day," and means, "Let's talk." He says, "I'm sure it was a breeze compared to yours," meaning, "Let's have sex." Both men and women in this situation may feel beleaguered, but men are much more likely to become—à la *Seinfeld*— irritable, irrational, and, yes, even desperate.

Those who study this phenomenon of sexual interest's variability are inevitably biased by their own sexual identity. I once received a news release from a major medical school and research center announcing "relief for menopausal women." It went on to say that "Menopausal women suffering from reduced sexual desire may find relief from an alternative type of hormone replacement therapy." The words suffering and relief in this context bothered me. The release noted further that "Women who took estrogen plus androgens reported improvement in libido and sexual satisfaction as early as three weeks after treatment began. . . . Their husbands reported the same thing." It made me wonder precisely whose sexual predicament was being studied, the women's or their husbands'.

The tendency to assume that a woman experiencing diminished interest in sex needs to be "fixed" is pretty pervasive. A few years ago, a male colleague sought my opinion about a patient who had come to see him because of her "decreased sexual drive." The patient was a woman in her midthirties who, after having been married for ten years, had a child, then a year later, a second child. She returned to work soon after the birth of each child, and, at the time she saw my colleague, was working full-time and mothering one- and two-year-old daughters. She reported being exhausted most of the time. This patient's husband was distressed because of his wife's disinterest in sex. Hence, her visit to the doctor.

After describing this social history, my colleague went through the unremarkable findings of the physical exam as well as the negative results of several lab tests. What, he wondered, did I make of this case. I told him I thought the diagnosis was in the first few sentences of the social history and that there was nothing wrong with this woman that some help from her husband and maybe a vacation wouldn't remedy.

A friend of mine was similarly stymied. She is an attractive, bright, socially competent woman whose fifteen-year marriage had been in bad shape for at least a few years, but probably since day one. From many conversations, I gathered that her husband had particular and frequent sexual needs that were not demonstrably accompanied by any particular tenderness or respect for her. Over the years she had undertaken couples counseling and read everything she could on the subject, conscientiously trying to understand her predicament. Despite all this, she called me one day to ask what she could take to improve her sexual desire. I told her I didn't think she needed improving.

Stories like these are legion. Men, women, and couples often hope to cast a woman's decreased libido in a medical framework in order to find a cure. I have yet to hear, however, of a male patient seeking to deamplify his libido to meet his partner's needs. As a culture, we hold tightly to the notion that the male sex drive is a given and that if any adapting is to be done, it must be done by women. How many men, after all, ever fake an orgasm?

The curious aspect of this cultural assumption is that only rarely do women's sexual impulses result in victimization. As a rule, women don't rape men, mothers don't molest their sons, women teachers and ministers don't accost those in their trust. When we elect our first woman president, her main problem is not likely to be a series of men emerging from the woodwork to accuse her of sexual harassment. The victimization from sexually aggressive women is sparse, that from male sexual aggression is vast. Still, we look to perk up the female's sex drive to accommodate the male's.

The consistent nature of the male sex drive can be thrown into bas relief by a marriage's political climate. It reminds me of the children's picture book, *If You Give a Mouse a Cookie* (Laura Numeroff, HarperCollins, 1985), wherein one thing always leads to another until you can hardly remember where it all began. When a woman is working full- or part-time, then coming home to do the lion's share of tending to the kids and household, she will inevitably become resentful—unless she thrives on being subservient or playing the martyr. When she is finally able to climb into bed at the end of a long day and evening, chances are she's not going to feel terribly amorous toward a partner who hasn't figured out how he might help. Remember, for her, sex is about emotional attachment and intimacy, while for him it needn't be. Her partner, in turn, becomes resentful about his wife's sexual reluctance. The two then wake up again the next day, feeling a bit better about one another because everything always looks better and brighter in the morning, but inevitably start the pattern all over again.

Whether there is a solution to the sexual discrepancies within many marriages is the million-dollar question. With the right therapist, couples counseling can be a valuable place to start. I believe coupons for marital therapy should be handed out with every marriage license. Having a neutral party available to moderate an exchange can allow each person to say things he or she may have been reluctant to say before for fear of provoking an argument. In this safe setting, communication skills that allow a topic to be defused before it is discussed can be practiced, and each partner can learn to ask for what he or she wants from the other person before becoming resentful because a need hasn't been anticipated. And just as a car needs a tune-up from time to time to keep it running smoothly, every marriage—especially when kids are part of the picture—can use a therapeutic intervention periodically.

Education is another approach—preventative premarital counseling, if you will. Why those who have been married for years just nod their heads at the assumptions inherent in courtship sex is perplexing. (Except perhaps because the male half of those long-time wedded couples don't tend to move beyond the courtship-sex mode.) It may not be possible to get single men and women to believe in the concept of marital sex as different from courtship sex, but with a little preparation, neither partner will feel betrayed when they confront the phenomenon.

The best solution to the common nonmeeting of married minds, however, lies generations in the future. When boys become men with radar sensitive to the demands of households and children, much of the marital dynamic will be different. "There are few things more sexy," I once heard a woman observe, "than a good father, a helpful husband, or a guy who is willing to put on an apron and give it his best effort." It's something to look forward to after *Seinfeld*.

Expect the Guilt Gap

One of the more subtle points that set mothers apart from fathers, not only in terms of their behavior but eventually in their children's minds, is their respective emotional proximity to guilt. "Show me a woman who doesn't feel guilty," said Erica Jong, "and I'll show you a man."

As we have seen, guilt has many guises. Useful guilt is internally generated based on a healthy sense of right and wrong learned in childhood; pseudoguilt is imposed by someone else's externally (or politically) generated notions of right and wrong; antiguilt is how we convince ourselves that guilt is not a useful sensibility.

The entire subject, at least as it pertains to women and children, stays at a pretty simple, external level for most men: simple no-nos generate simple guilt. Men seem to harken back to their childhoods and the scoldings they got from their mothers as boys when perceiving how things ought to be around a home. For example, Dad feels guilty when he promises the kid an afternoon at the zoo and reneges at the last minute. He feels guilty when he accidentally sticks the kid with a pin while changing his diaper (the reason we went to disposable diapers) and chastises himself for a whole hour before looking to see if he has been forgiven by his wife. He feels guilty when he returns home from a father–daughter outing with his toddler wearing only one of her brand-new $45 sneakers, or when he shows up late to the soccer game because he was playing tennis. He ostensibly feels so guilty, in fact, that he clears the table and cleans up the kitchen that night. A dad's mea culpas are often aimed at his partner and, while it gets the kitchen cleaned up from time to time, it leaves a guilt gap.

Women generally confront useful, internally generated guilt. Mom is motivated to make an arrangement more comfortable for her conscience and for her child, husband, or work situation—usually in that order. These different tendencies are one source of friction between mothers and fathers. Moms don't understand how dads can in good conscience not show up for, or even be late getting to, piano recitals, graduations, tiny-tot sports events, birthday parties, and other occasions that are important to children. Dads, on the other hand, don't quite get why mothers feel the need to honor so many kid occasions. Mothers consider the observance of these times as the right thing to do and feel guilty when they are not recognized. Dads—especially where young children are concerned—don't share the same innate sensibility about these occasions.

Another way of looking at the guilt gap is as follows: Mom wants a better/healthier/more workable situation for the family; Dad wants Mom to be happy so his sex life won't be negatively affected. Mom talks about feeling bad enough to do something to remedy the situation; Dad talks about being in the doghouse. And herein lies a large difference between mother guilt and father guilt.

An interesting thing happens, however, as children get older. Mom often quits playing the good cop as the kids become able to ask for what they want. I used to go crazy trying to get my husband to march in step with my guilt repertoire. One day I realized that I would never make him feel the way I do about holidays and special occasions. The best I could hope for was that he might take an interest of his own accord. At about the time I stepped back from trying to guilt-trip him into seeing things my way—a hopeless task when his conscience wasn't wired the same way as mine—the kids took up their own causes. He would, I realized, have to make his own way in forging relationships with his children.

The guilt gap stems largely from the freedom boys and men have enjoyed in not having to attend to the domestic aspect of their lives. Why would a person worry about a situation they know is being handled well? This phenomenon is hundreds of years old, making it impossible to guess at how long it might take to turn it around. Men, because they have not historically—or recently—been expected to bridge the chasm between the worlds of work and home, needn't think about whether the kids are getting enough fruits and vegetables, have a costume for the school play, have clean underwear for the next day, have toothpaste in their bathroom, or have made their beds when they leave for school. Fathers have the luxury of being able to compartmentalize what they need to worry about. Mothers, especially those who need to earn money, don't have this same leeway. The buck stops with their ability to notice and manage the myriad aspects of domestic life as well as the way it interfaces with life beyond the front door.

With the exception of a very unusual few, dads do not question whether to walk out the door to work each day or fret about which surrogate will replace him in his absence. Many dads assume that whatever they don't do their wife will, and whatever she can't do she will pay someone else to do, and whatever doesn't fall into those two categories isn't important. It must seem pretty simple. Yet in the gap left by dads' guiltlessness, many things accumulate. Responding to these can make the difference between a richly colored family life and one hastily sketched in black and white.

This knowledge that their husbands will not pick up where they leave off is what drives many professional women to the margins of their careers or back into their homes while their children are young. The knowledge that mothers will fill in the home front blanks as needed makes it easy for men to keep heading in their age-old directions, doing a little penance here and there and hoping for whatever forgiveness is necessary. Meanwhile, given these agendas, who can blame women for feeling enough guilt for both parents.

Question Kitchen Blindness

We all know the feeling. You're trying to get dinner on the table and the kids are at their hungry worst, whining and bickering incessantly. A telemarketer calls trying to get you to pledge money so sick children can have their dreams come true, and while you are on the phone the dog jumps up and in one gulp devours the last chunk of hamburger meat you left unpatted on the counter to answer the phone. With all this going on, you cover the receiver with your hand and turn to your husband who is sitting at the breakfast bar, oblivious to the chaos, reading the newspaper. "Would you put the ketchup on the table," you whisper encouragingly. While you are extricating yourself from the phone call as diplomatically as possible—because, after all, this isn't a magazine subscription drive—your husband stands before the refrigerator for what seems like an eternity, looking for the requested condiment. When you can finally hang up, you stride over to the fridge, reach to the nearest, clearest item on the top shelf, and bring your hand out with the family-size ketchup bottle. Your husband shrugs his shoulders in bewilderment. "Why couldn't I see that?" he wants to know.

He has what Nora Ephron referred to in her lightly concealed roman à clef, *Heartburn* (Pocket Books, 1983), as "kitchen blindness." No studies or major grants have investigated this phenomenon, but common knowledge puts the hereditary component of it somewhere on the Y chromosome. More than anything, however, kitchen blindness symbolizes a constellation of husband-like behaviors for which we have no scientific explanation. Things that fathers do that mothers joke about run a wide gamut: putting their daughter's dresses on backward; having to ask, "How many?" when apples appears on the grocery list; not knowing how to arrange for a baby-sitter; being incapable of talking on the phone while holding a baby; falling asleep halfway through any attempt to read a child a bedtime story; and wanting a guarantee that they will have a good time if they go to the friend's kid's birthday party. These have been the subject of Bombeckian commentary for decades.

While it's tempting to see these as culturally determined tendencies, their ubiquity together with the recent spate of scientific inquiry into the differences between men's and women's brains is enough to make you wonder if *la différence* isn't quite a bit more nature than nurture. Back in the seventies, besides thinking that we had it made in the professions, those of us coming into our childbearing years were convinced that all we had to do was give our sons dolls to play with and, voilà, they'd grow to be the good-hearted, equality-minded, kitchen-capable men we wish had been around when we were still single.

When I was twenty, I gave my eight-year-old sister a model airplane kit for Christmas, thinking to compensate for all the one-sided treatment she had, I was sure, been subjected to all her life. She ran from the room in tears when she opened it, and although I tried to console her, I was secretly convinced she would come around to my way of seeing things before long. I still cringe when I think about that episode, although it was not until I had children of my own that I fully realized the magnitude of my miscalculation. Whether by nature or nurture, by age eight my sister had long since gravitated away from any possibility of being interested in model airplanes.

Still pondering the role of cultural conditioning in determining gender roles, I bought a wooden train set, Transformers—the boy toy of the moment—and dolls for my first child, who was just toddling. She played with them all but none as enthusiastically or imaginatively as the dolls. When my son was born, the younger brother of two older sisters, no one needed to buy the kid any dolls. They were everywhere in our house. Still, as soon as he could crawl, he ferreted out not the dolls, but the basket containing the train set. He took great delight in tipping it over and making guttural noises. His first mission, once he could stand alone, was to bang the wooden track pieces on the coffee table (true distressed pine) and begin figuring out how to put them together. He was, as an observer once noted, born with an inner motor and went around for years sounding the part. Fortunately, I was so in love with him that his behavior, which took me completely by surprise after mothering two girls, didn't matter. It fell to this little guy to teach his mother about what makes the male of our species tick. I sometimes wonder how women without sons figure it all out.

Yet just as soon as we are becoming convinced that what makes fathers one way and mothers another is determined largely by genetics, we consider the men who make their money running housecleaning services, preparing meals for diners around the world, teaching children, or being firemen—in which job they must cook, clean, and walk the dog regularly. So, we think, men can clean, cook, and tend to domestic sorts of details without being begged, coaxed, nagged, or otherwise motivated against their will to do so—at least, that is, when the politics and remunerative potential of a given situation prescribe this behavior. In other words, when it is specified by a job description and rewarded with a paycheck.

Perhaps what's needed is a new domestic job description in more concrete terms. Where women once flooded into the sphere of work, studying and living up to job descriptions with great determination and skill, men—in a realm in which domestic labor is to be evenly apportioned—need to study and know quite intimately what's expected of them. The domestic job description cannot be pulled out the day after a wedding, however, and stand any chance of flying. Just as girls who grow to be income earners see this as their potential from the time they are very young and aspire to the expectations of the working world right alongside those of a household, so must men have this same dual outlook from an early age.

Still, this sounds a good deal simpler than it is. Both men and women regularly become stuck in a series of well-camouflaged traps that constitute the cultural roadblocks to accomplishing such domestic equality. From an early age, before we realize they are doing it, baby boys and girls observe the interaction between their parents. Not only do the boys identify with their dads and the girls with their moms, but both sexes integrate the observed interactions into their worldview. The same learning process that makes wife beating so stubbornly apparent in sequential generations of men accounts for kitchen blindness. Only considered in those terms, it's not so funny anymore.

Can this cycle be broken? Wife beaters, when identified in a fortunate manner, go to jail, participate in group therapy, and attend twelve-step programs, all of which doesn't always succeed in changing their behavior. What's learned young is learned well. To most reasonable observers, it would seem somewhat excessive to put men or women through such intensive behavior modification scenarios—Twelve Steps to Kitchen Vision—to change what, when said aloud, sound like trivial issues. Yet it is precisely the enormous range of these trivial issues that can make a marriage feel like political warfare.

The better and more thorough way to instill across-the-board domestic responsibility is to raise sons and daughters to help themselves, their parents, and one another in an ambiance of gender-neutral expectations. Everyone takes the garbage out, helps with kitchen cleanup, does their own laundry, and entertains the baby while Mom is fixing dinner. But the problem is that when it is Mom fixing dinner every night, the message sent about who should cook in a household is more powerful than any consciously designed effort to inspire gender neutrality in household matters. A son might do great things professionally with cooking talents derived from this background and still expect his wife to prepare meals at home.

Not only is this a frustratingly vicious cycle under the most favorable of circumstances, but there is no cultural agreement about what works best. Traditional domestic roles are still viewed as desirable in many spheres, though most women coming from such backgrounds will be expected to hold income-earning jobs at some time in their lives. Until competence in domestic matters is given the same cultural endorsement as professional competence, women and men will remain consigned to muddling along together and hoping for the best against many odds. Yet cultural endorsement is a tricky thing to come by, as those who would save our kids from things like tobacco have discovered. Not only do studies come and go giving us information without solutions, but when sufficient financial power supports a roadblock to sanctioning a code of behavior, it almost doesn't matter how much sense another viewpoint makes. And, at this writing, much money and power stands in the way of bringing men fully into the domestic realm.

Is there hope somewhere in all this for the current generation of girls, or are they destined to head into marriage and professional life in the same double bind as their mothers? The answer can only be guessed at. Certainly a generation spent observing their mothers' frustrations may point the next round of mothers in more well-thought-out directions. The answer also depends to a great extent on how much of a difference today's mothers are making, not just in raising their sons to be domestic helpers but in getting their husbands to model behavior that encourages sons in this direction. Many women are supporting this, trying their best to raise broad-minded, competent, good-hearted sons who will place as much value on their roles as fathers and keepers of the home as they do on their roles as breadwinners. But cultural changes happen about as quickly as dripping water contours a rock formation. Slowly, but we have to hope, very surely.

Shape the Future

One of the big differences between women with children and those without is what they want from their partners for their birthdays. Women without children want a gift, one that demonstrates some originality and thoughtfulness, as a show of appreciation and affection. Mothers want this too—of course, who wouldn't? But mothers will happily settle for just about anything as long as Dad sets a good example for his kids by doing something. I've never heard a man complain that his wife didn't set a good example for the kids by not coming through on his birthday. Mothers, however, for a variety of reasons that may have as much to do with fundamental differences between men and women as anything else we could talk about, take it much more than just personally when dads bungle birthdays.

And well they should. The daughter who watches her father take her mother for granted will grow up expecting nothing more from men. The son who watches Dad beg off on birthdays will have a ready-made repertoire of excuses for the special women in his life. And so it goes. This sort of learned, pernicious legacy, regardless of how inadvertent, becomes the baton we hand our kids to relay down the generations.

Unfortunately but practically, sons tend to be singled out as admirable projects for feminist moms. The current wisdom is that if we can teach these boys to be sensitive, caring, domestically competent men, our daughters will have it made in ways we wish we had. Saying this is one thing; putting it into practice is another thing altogether. We are mothers, after all, and these sons are our little guys. How far we go toward nurturing self-sufficiency in our sons may depend on how well we resist the maternal impulses that nudge us to make their lives too comfy.

A friend of mine whose husband died several years ago, and who has two teenaged sons, speaks poignantly on this subject. While she knows that many women in her situation would feel they had to be mother and father to the kids, she knows she is just Mom. And while she makes admirable efforts to keep them athletically active and in the hands of good male coaches, she doesn't feel compelled to play catcher to their pitches. This friend is a gentle, well-bred, soft-spoken woman who could easily cater to the "man" in each of her sons by taking care of all the messy details in their lives. Yet she tries to err on the side of being tough. They cook, clean, do laundry, go to the grocery store, and don't expect her to do for them what they can do for themselves. She encourages them to talk openly and frequently about their feelings and keeps a finger planted on the pulse of their progress in school. And she insists—keeping her sense of humor throughout—that they figure out gifts and special occasions to her satisfaction. Rather than trying to compensate in some way for the premature loss of their father by padding their lives with ease, privilege, or material comforts or by allowing them to be victims, she has nurtured their every strength, turning tragedy into triumph. In doing so she has honored their father's life and legacy.

Yet raising gracious, competent men is no easy feat. There is something about a son that can play a mother's heartstrings unmercifully if Mom is not careful. Despite girls' physical vulnerability relative to the other 49 percent of the population, I've always thought of my daughters as tough stuff. My son, on the other hand, aroused the overprotective parent in me from day one. Early in his preschool career, he earned the reputation of being a handful—Action Jackson they called him—and I hovered closely to make sure he was handled well. I watched from the corners of the classroom, went along on field trips, stayed for the duration of birthday parties, coached his first soccer team, and refused to allow him to be labeled or dismissed as a difficult child.

Sometimes I wonder if my attentiveness flowed more from fascination than from overprotectiveness. The two sisters who preceded him in the sibling lineup were the way I thought kids would be, which is to say they described an emotional trajectory with which I could identify. My son, on the other hand, was intense. Attention deficit hyperactivity disorder (ADHD) has an overly focused manifestation as well as its more well-known inattentive pattern, and watching my son lock onto a particular activity with all his neurological might sometimes made me worry that I was seeing the flip side of the attention deficit coin. Keeping in mind one of the guiding principles of parenting, that rather than intending a child to be a certain way you must discover who this small person actually is, I followed my son through early elementary school, discovering his personality as I went. This wasn't always a walk in the park; I had to keep him accountable while giving him enough rein to be a kid, and a male one at that.

There were times I thought I should give up hoping he would ever sit at a meal without spilling something, go to a party without sticking his fingers in the cake before it was cut, sit still during a stage performance, go into a toy store without having a tantrum over the toy gun I wouldn't buy, step back graciously from the plate after a third strike, or have his mind changed about anything he set it to. Expecting him to do the things his sisters did at the same age was a foolish proposition; he was not—I got it loud and clear—either of his sisters. But I never gave up my conviction that he is a great kid and will grow to be a wonderful man. To this day I keep treading that line between discovering who he is and nurturing who he can be.

One day when he was eight years old and I was waiting for his baseball practice to end, one of the fathers, also waiting by the fence, turned to me and said, "I want to tell you what a terrific son you have." I resisted an urge to hug this guy and smiled to myself for weeks thereafter. But that was just the first of many similar comments that coaches, teachers, and friends' parents have made over the last few years, a fortunate yardstick to have while my work is still in progress. And while many parents would have reached for Ritalin years ago in an effort to conform this child to their notion of who he should be, I was lucky to sense that what I was looking at wasn't abnormal, but rather a hearty manifestation of male development.

This isn't always the case. The concept of ADHD is still a constellation of symptoms, an imperfect estimation and not a measurable deficit. Parents can make one of two mistakes in assessing their child's need for treatment, both mistakes stemming from too much intention about who a particular kid should be: we can rush to medicate when some other sort of intervention is needed, or we can withhold medication when it is truly indicated. Either mistake does a disservice to the child. It helps, in making what is not always a clear choice, to remember that it is the parents' job to help their kid look good, not the child's job to make his parents look good.

Developing a sense about how best to nurture a son requires a mother's soft touch as well as her tough touch. What is often the most difficult part of the proposition is the time it takes—time to look closely, to imagine life through a boy's eyes, to be on hand when the steering needs to be done. And while this is true for girls, daughters are not as often the enigma for their mothers that sons are.

A child's potential is apparent at some level right from the start if someone takes the time to see it. The time I spent following and leading my son through his early years was validated along the way many times, but perhaps never as delightfully as when at age six he prodigiously sensed what would make my heart glad on a special occasion. With an originality, thoughtfulness, and affection I hope he will carry into his adult life, he commemorated an occasion with a gesture that even set a good example for his father. He made me a bookmark. On one side he drew a portrait of me with big buggy eyes, a huge smile, and hair down to my feet; on the other side, in his most careful penmanship he wrote, "happy mothers day; meny hogs and kisis; love G."

Mother's Day doesn't get any better.

Chapter Five

It's Not the Glass Ceiling, It's the Sticky Floor

Housekeeping ain't no joke.
—Louisa May Alcott

A family is much more than the sum of its parts. The interactions, relationships, and mechanics of day-to-day life are greater than Mom plus Dad plus Kid plus Kid. Keeping it all going in a positive direction requires the attention, in a big way, of someone—and in our culture, that someone is most often Mom. Even though this has been a fact of life for generations, it remains difficult for people other than mothers to comprehend the extent to which time and energy are routinely consumed by minutiae. It is even more difficult for nonmoms to acknowledge that much of this is crucial minutiae, the myriad little things that breathe life into the spirit of any family.

Get a Wife

One day when my youngest was eight years old, in one of those comments that seemed random but that I knew had been thought about for some time before it worked its way from her brain to her mouth, she asked me how I could do all the jobs I do. "What jobs are you thinking about?" I asked. "Well, you know," she replied still pondering the issue. "You have four jobs. You are a mother, a doctor, a column writer, and a soccer teacher." She paused as if to gauge whether she had covered it all, then added, "And you know, Mom, being a mother is a job."

"Yes indeed," I agreed. "Being a mother is a big job."

Several things about this exchange warmed my heart. First of all, in case I had ever wondered if anyone noticed what I did all day, I could now rest assured that I wasn't taken for granted. My eight-year-old was counting my vocations. More than that, however, this was a daughter beginning to sort out the possibilities open to her and taking notes about what uses up time in the space of a day. Most important, this little girl could see that being a mother wasn't a backdrop in the performance of adult life, but a large and definite part of the action.

The limits of the English language have been searched and found wanting on the subject of working mothers. All mothers work, some at home, others elsewhere; some gainfully and lots of others not so gainfully. We can talk about employed mothers, but it sounds awkward—awkward wording reflecting the awkwardness of the situation. Gainfully employed, working outside the home, working at home—although the IRS claims to know the difference, none of our semantic attempts to distinguish women's work from all other types of work really cut the mustard or ade-quately describe what it's called when you clean up the mustard.

I know this double bind. I have worked outside my home in a med-ical office, inside my home in a home office, outside my home taking care of family-related necessities, and inside my home doing the same. And while it doesn't all run together in a paycheck, it certainly does meld on my daily schedule as is illustrated by the following story of a day in the life.

It was one of those days that, to make myself maximally available but at the same time gainful, I had planned to spend working at home. Before I even made it to the coffeepot at 5:30 that morning, the tally of things to do, besides the gainful stuff on my desk, had already exceeded my capacity for mental enumeration. A list, I needed a list.

Over toast and grapefruit and between newspapers, I made notes to myself: mouse, rooster, phone calls, groceries—oh yeah, and work. I started by ignoring the list and walked the dog, emptied the dishwasher, folded a load of laundry, made school lunches, located a missing shoe, moderated a sibling dispute, and made sure all the kids had brushed their teeth before heading to the car and two separate schools. Of course, three hours of nonstop activity into the day, I hadn't yet begun to work. That came next.

Returning from school drop offs, I headed directly to my home office. A few minutes into my gainful employment, I discovered my fax machine wasn't cooperating with my plan for the day. Since this machine helps my home office endeavors to be considered work, I had to stop everything and attend to it. Alas, when you work at home, you can't call your assistant from another room to handle electronic failures just because they bring your gainful efforts to a screeching halt.

As I was unplugging the fax, I noticed the mouse from my early morning list sitting alongside my keyboard. This was not a family pet, but another piece of faulty electronic equipment—the mouse from the kids' computer that my oldest daughter had put where she was hoping I wouldn't miss it.

Just as I was beginning to feel discouraged by the large glitch the fax failure presented to what I had hoped would be a gainful kind of day, I was stirred from my disheartening contemplation by the boisterous cock-a-doodle-dooing of the rooster—that's right, the one from the list—in the backyard. This bird was supposed to have been a hen, but whoever was doing the chick sexing the day this bird's number came up, goofed. This loud red "foul" was on my list because I needed to find him a home out-side the city limits, away from my bedroom window and my neighbors' nerves. Unlike the well-behaved farmyard roosters in my kids' picture books, this one crowed at any hour of the day or night making everyone in the vicinity, myself included, less gainful for lack of sleep. He was going to be tricky to catch, however, so I decided to leave him until later.

Before I set out to do electronic-repair rounds, I made a few phone calls, some gainful, others not so gainful, all necessary. I called a couple of patients with their lab results, RSVPed to a parents' meeting at one of the schools, phoned my newspaper editor to beg deadline mercy, made several dental appointments for the kids, and called the team mom of the soccer team I coach to ask her to call everyone else with game-time info. Finally, four hours into the morning, I had actually accomplished something. By this time I scarcely cared whether or not it paid.

I headed to the car. The fax machine and I went to Sam's Electronics, the mouse and I went to the computer store (love that extended warranty), and the rooster got a reprieve. It became apparent soon into this run around town, however, that when the car brakes had been "fixed" the day before, something hadn't been adjusted quite right. A tremendous shaking seized my sport utility vehicle whenever the speedometer exceeded thirty-five miles per hour. The car and I went to Albert's.

"Two hours" was the bad news from Albert about how long he would need the car. Now I was really discouraged, but since the service station was across the street from the grocery store, I could at least use the kink in my schedule to address the mounting complaints at home that "there's nothing to eat." After filling two grocery carts with stuff I hoped would qualify as things to eat, I retrieved the car, loaded the bags, and headed home.

By the time the groceries were all put away, the in-home working part of my day was over, poof. It hadn't been very productive from a gainful point of view, but time is time and when it's up, it's up. Launching into the nonworking, out-of-home part of my day, I set off to get the kids from school and address their requests for after-school snacks. This done, we headed off to the piano lesson, hockey rink, and dentist's office, first going one direction to drop off, then reversing the order to pick up.

Next came the nonworking, in-home interval that includes dinner, homework (love that new mouse), more dishes, more laundry, and bed-time routines. This section was bumped back when my son discovered that he had left his shoes (call me stupid, but they were his only pair) at the hockey rink. Since I don't get paid any more to cry than to laugh, I took a deep breath, left the pasta to congeal in its pot, and drove the five miles to fetch the shoes. (The IRS may be able to detect differences in all this, but I haven't learned to yet.)

Where, you ask, was my husband in all this? Why working, of course. And where would our family be if I were trying to do the same things with my days that he does with his? I can't answer that, but I have a rea-sonably good feeling that it wouldn't be pretty. Managing the diffuse, unpredictable, and reasonable needs of a home and children is work, and someone has to do it.

As I was nodding off midsentence in *The Indian in the Cupboard* and my son was shaking me and saying, "Mommy, read," I experienced a moment of panic about how little I had accomplished that day. I needed help but it would have to be a wife because, let's face it, if you call an all-purpose assistant anything else, he or she costs too much. Of course, it might be worth it. I could sit at my desk, feeding my fax machine, hitting those deadlines, and attending to patient charts knowing that someone else, some truly valuable person, would go out in the backyard and catch the darn rooster.

Sweat the Small Stuff

"Hail, ye small sweet courtesies of life! for smooth do ye make the road of it," wrote Laurence Stern in 1768. The passing of two centuries has reduced this observation to a simpler, less sweet form for which Mr. Stern is never accorded credit: It's the little things in life that count.

No sooner are we done contemplating this essential component of any interpersonal arena, however, than we are admonished not to sweat the small stuff, and further, asked to believe that it's all small stuff. So which is it anyway? Do we take good care of the trivia trove comprising our day-to-day needs and interactions, or do we shrug our shoulders at the same time we shrug off any responsibility for the details?

A mother asks herself this question a million times a day. She wonders this as she sprinkles pumpkin-shaped pasta into boiling water for children who may or may not even notice. She wonders this as she tucks a favorite snack item into a child's lunch sack; as she shops for gifts, groceries, and clothing, making good choices because she clocks the preferences; as she feeds the forgotten goldfish, catches the fugitive hamster, or chases the unwanted rooster. She wonders this as she walks the dog, knowing that waiting for someone else to do it can result in sweating rather unpleasant stuff. She wonders all this only for a minute, however, because she senses that although staying abreast of the little things is a niggling job, somebody's got to do it (and because at least the dog is appreciative).

Trifling it is, yet the story of the better part of my life—and here I'm speaking both quantitatively and qualitatively—could be told through the small stuff that both consumes and rewards it daily. Is there milk for cereal in the morning, has the field-trip permission slip been signed, did I remember to pick up the dry cleaning, will I be back in time to greet the appliance repairman, and is today the appointment with the vet? If I were to put a job title on what I do with the portion of my time that my husband wonders about, I'd call myself a Small Stuff Technician. Who else keeps track of whether there is school on Friday, whether there is salt in the water softener, what happened to the new golf glove, when the library books are due, what's for dinner tonight, and how much of our family's fundraising commitment we've worked off in grocery script? The cogs and wheels that move a family forward from one day to the next would come to a gnarled halt were it not for the grease applied by the Small Stuff Technician.

Once upon a time, big things and little things were more easily defined and assigned. Women attended to the "small sweet courtesies of life," while the men in our midst didn't sweat the small stuff (and it was all small stuff). Now that the old division of labor has been abolished—from a theoretical standpoint—and replaced by a more random and vague if less arbitrary notion of who does what, who is supposed to step up with pride to mind the minutiae?

This question runs around unchecked, unbridled, and without direction in many marriages. That the answer has enormous consequences is rarely considered. Some of the best things in life—children, pets, gardens, houses, and hobbies—create a dense subterranean layer of trivia requiring frequent, albeit seemingly inconsequential, dedications of time, thought, and energy. Insufficient respect for the Small Stuff Technician's role would have life transpire in the absence of those things that make it all worth living. Why bother with a family that has no kids, dogs, backyards, homes, or recreational pursuits.

Striking a harmonious division of labor is not often a happy undertaking and is indeed the stuff of marital strife, not to mention sibling rivalries. Whose turn is it anyway to write thank-you notes for mutual gifts, make the bed, take out the garbage, or—hey kid!—walk the dog. Some folks just keep at it by trial and error until a workable system emerges. Others debate these things until they die. And the most desperate call upon science to validate their pathetic positions, citing the different biological imperatives of men and women.

All this means that the ability to spot-treat stains, remember who doesn't like nuts in their brownies, memorize the baby-sitter's telephone number, and remember that toilet paper is needed even when it's not on the grocery list, while once acknowledged appreciatively if not monetarily, involves talents residing in the twilight zone of human accomplishments. These skills do nothing for a résumé but are essential for civilized survival. Never mind that acclaimed scientists, artists, politicians, and literary figures are, in the name of the big stuff, forgiven gross incompetence in the realm of practical life achievements. Someone has to handle their dirty laundry.

I contemplate these things secretly because, although I am, by tacit understanding if not twisted arm, the Small Stuff Technician in our home, too much discussion of the matter can take the "sweet" out of the courtesy. My family, whether they say it out loud or not, clearly delights in the little things and will appreciate the designer pasta if it doesn't get soggy while I'm feeling put-upon. Is it a big deal or a little deal to pay attention to such detail? I don't know and don't tell anyone I asked. Just say, the goldfish wanted to know.

Teach Your Children Well

Most women, when asked after ten years of marriage and motherhood whether their original expectations correlate with their current reality, hardly know where to begin to describe the disconnect. The distance defies easy description. "Never in my wildest imaginings . . ." is about as close as most can get toward articulating the extent to which they have adjusted their premarital fantasies to fit their current situation. The unanticipated comeuppances and triumphs, heartbreaks and joys, pain and delight, constitute nothing less than a Ph.D. in life's lessons.

The class schedule to which most women adhere while obtaining this degree changes daily. Nursing mothers are required to attend middle-of-the-night sessions on patience, face biological challenges like sleep deprivation, and tolerate postponed gratification. Mothers of preschoolers are expected to have done their homework, including voluminous reading about child psychology. An exam question that could require a different answer every day for six months might be, "Why is my three-year-old so much more of a challenge now than when she was two?" (Hint: The terrible twos are a myth.)

By the time the teen years roll around, a mother needs to have completed oral exams in how to manage temper flares, inspire cooperation (against all odds), motivate good judgment, and prevent teen pregnancy. These oral exams are performed as a mother dashes around town and waits for kids to finish various lessons and activities, all the while talking to herself. The unavoidable interactions—or altercations, as the case may be—with her instructors, the children, also qualify as verbal evidence of evolving motherly competence. The paper trail leading to this Ph.D. may be sparse, but the resulting education beats Ivy League hands down.

The family, as an institute of higher learning, imparts its wisdom to those who spend the most time navigating its ever-changing course requirements. The parent who goes the patient distance in discussing the responsibilities that come with the privilege of having car keys, and gets the point across, makes the grade, momentarily anyway. Taking up each issue as it comes along—from toddler temper tantrums to television time to teenage temperance—is a relentless, sometimes thankless, and occasionally rewarding process. Like much else about marriage and parenthood, it takes leaps of faith to keep at it when any even remote glimmers of gratification are nowhere in sight.

More important than anything parents ever say, however, is the behavior they model. It does no good to give the good-driver rap while cruising through stop signs, driving after drinking alcohol, or leaving seat belts unused. Every parent would love to think their children will do as they say, not as they do, but that would be entirely too easy. Any parent can say, "Hey, kid, be a good person," and then go right on being a jerk. But jerks tend to beget jerks.

Every set of parents home schools their children. It doesn't matter how much time a child spends in school or a parent spends at work each day. Nor does it matter how much tuition is paid toward formal schooling. Children take the bulk of their cues from their parents and home situation. They may learn that two plus two equals four for the purpose of a second-grade math quiz. The two-plus-twos of everyday life—personal relationships and character—however, are mastered at home. Every interaction, every answer to every question, the way every crisis or mundanity is handled, the extent to which a parent is physically and emotionally available—all of these accumulate in layers and launch kids accordingly.

At its best, the family as an institute of higher learning does two things besides confer degrees in practical wisdom on parents: it inspires children with a lifelong love of learning, and it teaches them emotional intelligence. To accomplish the former, parents have to provide an educational ambiance, model desirable behavior, have high expectations, and take genuine pride in their children's achievements. Providing hands-on help with homework, leading the way in dinnertime discussions, being the first to forego television, and setting standards by example will teach more effectively than will any number of lectures on how to succeed. Story after rags-to-riches story gives credit to the inspiration provided by a parent or parents, even in the face of overwhelming odds, as the main ingredient in success. Moreover, a common theme emerging from many retrospective accounts recognizes the home environment and formal education roles as synergistic.

Besides its role in according due respect to the three Rs, however, the importance of family and home life in developing an individual's emotional IQ is gaining recognition. And as with all elements of learning, the earlier that emotional intelligence is fostered, the more adept a child will be at utilizing his or her emotional capabilities. An emotionally intelligent child becomes good at reading the interpersonal dynamics in various situations, at valuing the feelings of others, and at gauging how their own emotions affect their performance. They are empathetic; have good impulse control; are likable, adaptable, and friendly; and command respect. But although the elements of this emotional competence come naturally to most kids, these elements need to be reinforced and encouraged at an early age in order to grow up with the child.

Since Daniel Goleman popularized the concept of emotional intelligence several years ago in his book of the same name, more attention is being paid to this aspect of education. Some schools have introduced programs into their curriculums that are geared to teaching emotional awareness and to raising their students' emotional quotients. The increasing body of evidence supporting this effort's value shows that children who are very successful only in a strict academic sense do not do as well with success and happiness as those who also have high emotional IQs.

The child who loves to read will likely do well in school. But the child who loves to read and knows how to handle adversity will stand a better chance of doing well throughout life.

Because the family is an institute of higher learning, the two concepts of academic and emotional competence merge naturally and unremittingly at home. This means parents are on call as academicians day and night. From the time a two-year-old asks, "Why?" to the time a teenager asks, "Why not?" parents are required to be at their smartest. But just when a parent thinks her job as teacher is done for the day, she will be called upon to moderate a sibling dispute, impose discipline, or help guide a child through an emotional meltdown. Then, as always, that parent will give her child two answers: the thing she says and the thing she does. And for most women, those things change as they too become smarter and emotionally wiser, while progressing toward obtaining advanced degrees in managing marriage and motherhood.

Savor Uncomfortable Moments

Raising children is largely a matter of coming to terms with the imagined versus the real, the latter involving some uncomfortable moments which the former is spared. Hollywood and parenting literature don't prepare us for the reality warp that exists between what is supposed to happen and what ultimately does occur when it comes to kids, spouses, homes, pets, or just about anything else on which mothers rivet their attention.

My kids, for instance, being normal products of their era and environment, love home videos. So taken are they by these soon-to-be-obsolete entities that one or two movies invariably end up in the grocery cart as I wend my way past strategically placed video display cases. Because I am ordinarily oblivious to the videos amidst the victuals until we reach the checkout counter, one or another of the kids frequently gets sent packing to return the movie to the shelf from whence it came. Occasionally I'll give in to pleas for movie mercy, but only when the price sticker is less than fifteen dollars. In this case I allow the movie to be loaded into a sack alongside the groceries because, as I'm painfully aware after all these years, I can't rent it for this price.

Well, okay, technically I could rent it for less than three dollars a day.

In reality, however—and this is where all the advice literature falls apart— I would rent the movie, the kids would watch it more than once, the tape would stay in the VCR, the cover would slip under the couch, and a week later I'd get a call from the video store reminding me, in an uncomfortable moment, that said video was still lurking somewhere around my home.

In my own defense let it be said that sometimes I'm more organized than this. Sometimes I actually put the video in the car after it's been viewed once, so I'll remember to return it promptly the following day. Despite feeling self-righteous not to mention virtuous when I operate this way, I still get that call from the video store a week later. I then have to do a thorough search of the car for the movie, which, predictably, slipped under a seat the minute I placed it in the car and promptly became out of sight and out of mind. Having to grope around in the muck that collects under car seats until my sensory-motor skills tell me that the shape in my hand is the missing video and not a missing library book is only part of the price paid for renting the video in the first place.

In the event that a video winding up in my grocery cart is not only dirt cheap but family fare, my tolerance for price goes up even higher. Cheap in this case is rarely dear. I remember, in particular, picking up a new copy of *Mrs. Doubtfire* some years ago for $9.99. (Actually, I didn't pick it up; the kids picked it up and snuck it into the grocery cart.) What I love about family movies is that, not only can everyone watch them, but they paint pictures for my kids of how family life might be on another planet.

Take, for instance, the scene in *Mrs. Doubtfire* in which Miranda (the mom, played by Sally Field, aka Gidget) is going to interview the nanny candidate, Mrs. Doubtfire. "C'mon," she says buoyantly to her three kids who, we are supposed to believe, are really no different than mine, "I want you to meet the new baby-sitter and tell me what you think" (or something to that effect). The kids line up and courtesy prevails until the oldest daughter protests having to have a baby-sitter in lieu of the father's presence. This mild outburst appears to be an uncomfortable moment for the mother. When I saw this I thought, Miranda (Gidget), honey, you ain't seen nothin' if you think that's uncomfortable.

Mentally moving from Hollywood to reality, I recalled the evening a new sitter came to our house to be interviewed and meet my kids. During this interview, my five-going-on-fifteen-year-old made rhymes with any obscene word she could think of, and though she hadn't the faintest notion of what she was saying—except for it being a tried and true attention grabber—her not-so-Mother-Goosey poetry caused the college-age baby-sitter to blush. (Mrs. Doubtfire never blushed about anything.)

In the meantime, my nine-year-old ran in, let loose several inflated balloons, and yelled, "Fart," as they sputtered around the room backward. My efforts at recovering any decorum were met with swift and terrible defeat when my twelve-year-old quite solemnly slid into place alongside me on the couch with two enormous balloons stuffed under her shirt. Ahem, may I present the children.

Needless to say, when the twenty-one-year-old interviewee negotiated all this with smiling aplomb, I hired her on the spot. I remembered why I once wanted to stay twenty-one for the rest of my life and remain in that twinkling between vividly knowing what it was like to be a kid and having the privileges of adulthood, but not yet having to be the mom.

At times I try to remove myself to that place again. In restaurants, for instance, when a child's behavior is raising eyebrows at other tables, it's tempting to say, in a voice that can be heard by all onlookers, "You know, your mother wouldn't like that if she were here." This line comes in handy when my older two throw food, my son burps loudly, or my youngest plucks the largest strawberries from my fruit cup to use for nostrils on her Mickey Mouse pancakes. Though I'm a firm believer in the logical consequence school of discipline, the most logically consequential thing I can think to do at times like these is pretend they are someone else's kids.

Restaurants, in fact, are the scene of many an uncomfortable moment; you must be powerfully optimistic to venture into restaurants with children. One New Year's morning I took my younger two kids out to breakfast and had to wait for a table. Another lobby-bound woman smiled at my five-year-old, complimenting her on the dress she wore. "I slept in it," replied my daughter cheerfully, then having been put in mind of the prior evening's bedtime offered matter-of-factly, "I didn't brush my teeth last night either."

For a moment I hoped someone would say, "Cut," and the whole scene would turn out to be a movie. But, alas, it was too real and unscripted—not to mention uncomfortable—for Hollywood. It's at times like this, when what is supposed to happen eludes what actually transpires, that—movies and parenting advice aside—sometimes even mothers blush.

Chapter Six

Money Is a
Many-Splendored Thing

*Indeed, I thought, slipping the silver into my purse, it is remarkable,
remembering the bitterness of those days, what a change of temper a
fixed income will bring about.*

—Virginia Woolf

Money isn't everything. Alone it can't buy
health, marital happiness, psychological fitness, or
well-adjusted kids. Still, when financial anxiety permeates a
family's existence, it will invariably affect all these things
adversely. Striking a prudent truce between income and
spending can be tricky, particularly because time spent on
"women's work" is not a breadwinning proposition, and because
there is no sure formula for anticipating a family's needs as it
grows and becomes more complex. In the long run, the way a
family balances its time and money will paint a portrait more
telling than any other family picture.

When Equality Bites, Bite Back

We had high hopes. The heady days of sixties and seventies feminism promised those of us coming of age a chance to follow in our father's footsteps, not just our mother's. The objectives seemed so fair, so reasonable, so obvious. We expected equal pay for equal work—a no-brainer in anyone's book. We expected to be judged on our merits, not on our looks. And we were fully convinced that once we had these things—and most of us at some point thought we already did—our sexual perspectives would differ not at all from those of the men in our lives. The whole era lifted off like a Concorde jet, optimistically hoping to reach its destination in record time. After a spectacular takeoff, however, it began to experience insurmountable delays. For the most part, the concept of equality, even thirty years later, continues to circle various landing strips, parachuting out a brave soul now and then, and waiting for clearance to land. The women piloting the plane, after showing remarkable dexterity with the takeoff controls, have not been able to communicate effectively with the tower because the tower, it turns out, is occupied by men. And men, our pilots have discovered to their dismay after flying around for decades, are using a different directional codebook than either the pilots or the passengers. The tower says, "You're cleared for landing," and the women look down and say, "That's nice, but this plane won't fit on that landing strip." This state of affairs isn't necessarily by anyone's deliberate design, but rather it is a glaring mutual miscalculation.

Although some of these "miscalculations" are not really much different than they were three or four decades ago, many things have changed. Then, women had more difficulty receiving serious consideration for responsible positions because the male gatekeepers for those positions believed that women were less likely to toe the line than their male counterparts. It was assumed that motherhood would eventually derail even the most promising women. Given this eventuality, it seemed the better part of wisdom to invest education and training in men, not women.

Feminism took aim at this presumption, and if it did nothing else—although it did plenty more—it effectively deconstructed the acceptability of this type of thinking. Even if a college recruiter, graduate school dean of admissions, law partner, or CEO felt this way, it became deplorable to admit it. Women, at the same time, took on the task of proving themselves as equals among men in the professions. Motherhood, as predicted, threw up enormous obstacles to these women's abilities to walk in men's shoes.

Take breast-feeding as an example. During the fifties and sixties, because much less was recognized about the nutritional virtues of breast milk, mothers who procured jobs away from their homes didn't agonize over their baby's nourishment since formula was thought to be at least as nutritionally sound as breast milk, if not more so. As the story unfolded to reveal how much more breast milk provides than just calories—antibodies, protection against infectious disease, higher IQs, better academic performance even into the teen years, and emotional bonding—women wiggled around uncomfortably trying to align this information with what the male workplace expected from them. Nursing mothers were not accommodated in the workplace. To this day, many nursing mothers are relegated to bathrooms or other less than ideal settings to pump their breasts during lunch or coffee breaks so they can keep their infants optimally nourished and continue working.

When I went back to finish my medical school clerkships after Vanessa was born, I carried a pager. Because it was a hospital setting, I was able to wear this electronic leash inconspicuously and dash out periodically to nurse my baby. Some years later, when Galen was tiny, my sitter would deliver him to me at least once during my fourteen-hour stints at a clinic in a neighboring town. I learned to configure my own situation, but it would have been much less nerve-racking to have the blessings of the medical establishment and not merely the winks of a few kindly colleagues while I was doing so.

Not to be discouraged, women went clunking around in men's shoes, padding blisters and tripping with great regularity until they discovered they could wear their own shoes and still get the job done. Maybe they didn't need to be a senior partner; maybe an outpatient clinic was a better fit for a woman physician than private practice; perhaps work could be taken home or be done by more than one person. This collective epiphany, that women should approach the workplace on their own terms, is only now, thirty plus years into the great social experiment begun by the sixties feminists, gaining acceptance. That large corporations everywhere are vying for the title of most "family friendly" is evidence of this.

In the long run, official corporate attitudes are important, but so are the attitudes of the individuals with whom one works. I was fortunate to come across several helpful male colleagues while fighting my uphill battle to combine medical school, marriage, and pregnancy. One of these colleagues was the dean of students at my medical school, a man who played "Dad" to our entire class, admonishing us from the first day to "work hard, play hard." Since he had counseled me on classes and clerkships, I naturally conferred with him about how to arrange my fourth year around my pregnancy and due date. I had a six-week vacation saved up in anticipation of the baby's arrival and was terribly anxious about the timing of things. This kind counselor informed me that primips (first-time moms) almost always deliver late and advised me to schedule my vacation about ten days after my due date, which I did. Vanessa cooperated nicely and arrived on the last day of my internal medicine clerkship—the day before my vacation began.

Still, while enlightened corporate positions and personal allies can remove even large obstacles to women's professional aspirations, these tell only a fraction of the whole story. Feminism, while looking pretty comprehensive during the sixties, took aim at only one side of the inequality problem. With tremendous uneasiness, it began to dawn on the women who moved en masse into the workforce during the seventies and eighties that their freedom to work was not accompanied by the same freedom from domestic considerations as was their husband's freedom to work. While eight hours at the office for men was followed by a dinner prepared by someone else and a stint in an easy chair in front of the tube, women went and still do go home after their nine-to-fives to fix those dinners, wash dishes, help with homework, and do a couple of loads of laundry, all while taking the family's pulse. This domestic double standard, as many women can testify, breeds resentment.

Even if women were now receiving equal pay for doing precisely the same work as their male counterparts in every arena—which they are not—they are paying a higher price at home. This figures out to a net deficit for mothers relative to fathers. Nonetheless, in the absence of either an official dollar figure or a solid cultural agreement about the value of domestic efforts, neither of which is anywhere on the horizon, this work gap will not go away any time soon. My daughters will likely face the same assumptions about family work that every other woman leading up to their generation has: this work is good, necessary, commendable, and time consuming but, because it has no tangible worth, it remains valuable only to those who perceive its value. As a society, we are notoriously imperceptive on this count.

It's a curious predicament, however. The original deal specified equal pay for equal work, which seemed ambitious enough at the time. The codicil being added after the fact, always a more difficult way to accomplish something, specifies equal pay for all paid work and equal participation in all unpaid work, the latter being domestic work. This is doubly problematic. Not only is the deal being amended, but the amendment requires that men—and not just those holding the corporate purse strings and decision-making power—make compromises, and unglamorous ones at that. It's one thing to get the institutional support of the generals, to get a company or law firm or astronaut program to step up to a more favorable public profile by including women. It's quite another to get the foot soldiers who have been accustomed to having things done for them— underwear washed, kids cared for, refrigerators stocked, and bathrooms cleaned—to make the necessary adjustments. The guys in the former category feel virtuous; those in the latter category feel put upon. This means that not only are wives feeling resentful, but husbands are too. The family's pulse in this scenario becomes, as we say in medical circles, weak and thready. As a result, we as a nation have been standing by to commence CPR on the family.

Yet the best therapeutic options to remedy this situation are not clear. Occasionally an article shows up on a newspaper's feature page citing a study about the uneven division of home labor. The topic isn't very sexy and tends to hold up a societally unflattering mirror. Some progress has been made, we are inevitably told, and interviews are cited to support this notion. Yet the vast majority of mothers reading these stories shake their heads and wonder where is the equality of work in their homes.

Some savvy nouveau couples, recognizing the amount of time that will be necessary to raise a family, strike mutually acceptable deals. Some agree to take the traditional road while their children are young, freeing up the woman to care for the home while the man brings in the old-fashioned bacon. So long as both parents agree to this arrangement, it can work splendidly. Others set out to achieve a more "liberated" scenario and decide to divide both home and work labor down the middle. This is a tricky proposition because of the never-ending negotiation required to pull it off and because standards may differ between the parents. Many couples apply this equal-time standard to two full-time jobs, which, with a child or two in the picture, usually means full-time stress as well. And a few pioneer couples have turned tradition on its head by sending the woman to work while the man stays home with the children. Given mutual respect, this can work as well as the reverse because it recognizes the time and attention required by hearth, home, and kids. Not many couples opt for this approach because it rarely suits both the father's and the mother's fancy. Perhaps more tellingly, even stay-at-home dads tend to revert to traditional roles when Mom walks in.

Take my good friend who, with her husband and small children, comes to stay with my family each summer for a couple of weeks. This woman works three-quarters time in an office job that requires a fair amount of traveling. Her husband, meanwhile, does freelance consulting out of their home. He takes the two children to preschool each morning and retrieves them at noon. He orchestrates naps and afternoon activities and does some of the grocery shopping. When my friend comes home in the late afternoon, she prepares dinner and handles baths and bedtimes while her husband puts in a couple more work hours. I've always viewed theirs as close to an ideal arrangement.

There are, however, several chips in the polish on this story. My friend has an ongoing—albeit low-level—heartache about not being able to spend more time with her kids. She is chronically tired and stressed and has, as time wears on, given up more and more of her exercise time to make things work. Still, any situation with children demands sacrifice. The part that has always puzzled me has to do with what she says almost every time they arrive from the East. She laughingly notes that in preparation for these trips, her husband packs his bag and says, "Let's go," while she scrambles to make sure the kids' clothes, transition objects, diapers, bottles, car seats, and portable cribs are clean and packed. Working into the wee hours the night before they leave, she has to anticipate all the vagaries of traveling with kids, and this despite the fact that he is in many ways the primary kidcare person in their family equation. She always arrives exhausted.

The great preponderance of stories I hear from working women suggests this is by no means an isolated phenomenon. Like the polar opposite ends of magnets, mothers and fathers seem to come only so close to meeting one another halfway before something starts to jiggle out of alignment. Standing by itself, the original goal of equal pay for equal work is a great deal closer to becoming a reality as a result of feminist efforts. The notion that the same equality should extend to domestic endeavors, however, has a long way to go, much farther than any institutional solution can reach. In the context of the workplace, equality has many marshals standing at the ready to ensure compliance and, therefore, has made steady progress in traditionally male and corporate settings everywhere. Nonetheless, once the discussion moves from the public to a private setting, all bets are off and a woman is on her own to negotiate the best deal for herself in the face of long-standing cultural obstacles. The same woman who argues a case in front of a jury and gets a favorable verdict for her client may not win a personal success in the courtroom of hearth, home, and husband.

The cultural tenacity of domestic roles goes a long way toward keeping women's careers from rising along the same trajectory as men's. A certain amount of insidious institutional sexism may linger here and there and occasionally prevent a woman from ascending to a traditionally male-held position. More often, however, one's performance, not one's gender, is the gold standard on which promotion is based. Things that get in the way of performance, then, will ultimately sabotage a person's chances for advancement. For fathers, performance at work has traditionally been cut loose from home duties and responsibilities, whereas for mothers, no such unconditional freedom exists. The ability to commit to extra hours and weekend work, to remain focused on a project at work without peripheral distractions or interruptions, to be predictably in attendance, to be able to drop everything else on a moment's notice, to make work the priority— all these recommend a person for promotions. Yet most women with children are not likely to compare favorably with their male colleagues on these counts.

Some people see this discrepancy as a misogynistic conspiracy aimed at keeping women out of positions of power. Yet this way of thinking assumes some sort of collaborative, intentional effort involving men against women. It's much more likely, if not more obvious, that both men and women are subject to their society's cultural norms, and that rearranging these requires an effort—not only a permissive stance, but a real effort—from both. In order to gain admission to formerly off-limits careers, women made an untenable deal: They offered to work like men and hoped (not part of the deal) that things at home would somehow be handled. That this didn't happen has to do with the faulty nature of the original deal. Women wanted equal pay for equal work without understanding that access to that equal pay depended on their ability to do that equal work in as unfettered a way as men do their work. Until men are willing to do equal work at home, or pay someone to do that work, women—even those who are ready to make the necessary trade-offs—will remain at a distinct disadvantage and seldom be able to commit to their careers unconditionally.

The notion that all work, including domestic work, deserves equal pay and requires equal participation has a long way to go. Women's careers are dragged down by their domestic lives, preventing women who truly want to do so from rising to the upper echelons of their professions. The glass ceiling exists, not necessarily because of any misogynistic conspiracy, but because working women with children, unlike working men with children, are seldom able to commit to their careers unconditionally.

Give Yourself Credit

Financial worry causes the single greatest stress on most marriages. When a breadwinner loses a job, when the bills pile up, when the taxes exceed the accountant's estimate, or when the roof starts to leak, nothing, not even sex, will make everything all right until the family ledgers are in balance again. Even before any bad news or catastrophe, however, just making ends meet on a daily basis requires two incomes for many families and can stretch not only the couple's financial but their emotional reserves. But this is only part of the real picture.

Sometime during the past two decades we went from being a society that, for the most part, sent one member of a couple off to make money and kept the other one home to look after the kids, to being a society that sends both parents out to drum up income. There is, given this shift in who goes where to do what, an attention deficit on the domestic front. This void, which was once filled by extended family members, has been filled more recently by surrogate caregivers who go by a variety of names: baby-sitters, nannies, au pairs, preschools, and daycare centers. Some of these serve the purpose nicely, and some don't.

Despite the claims of many a sociologist, not to mention those of the religious right, the factors that conspired to create two-income imperatives for families are complex. It wasn't that self-centered women abandoned drab domestic futures for corporate boardrooms in a wholesale manner, thereby leaving children in the clinch. Even if we were to believe that rationale, the next logical inquiry would be, where were the dads?

In our sound-bite world of explanations, we are often only permitted one quick, shallow, catchy phrase with which to tell long, complicated stories. That economic tranquillity was more apparent than real during those years—when the cost of the American Dream rose steadily and families went from spending one-fourth of one person's income on housing to spending one-fourth of two people's income on housing—doesn't get talked about. It's much more juicy to say that all those terrible women who cared more about their ambitions than they did about their families are to blame for the ills of the family than it is to dissect the problem layer by layer. (And besides, what about those dads?)

Women's move into the workplace, for whatever reason you believe this happened, involved a large rearrangement of who was valued for what. In an economy that assesses itself only by the health of its gross domestic product (GDP), a huge pool of labor—domestic labor—gets ignored. It's possible, then, to take the country's temperature and get encouraging readings that are deceptive; a large aspect of the health and well-being of our system isn't measurable by conventional (read monetary) means. If every child who had emotional problems because of divorce, poor schooling, large amounts of unsupervised time alone, poverty, or discrimination registered negatively on the GDP, we might address these problems sooner and more effectively.

It doesn't help that we are politically schizophrenic about who should work and who shouldn't. When, in 1997, a professional couple in New England pressed charges against their teenaged British nanny for the death of their young son, a vicious outpouring of blame was witnessed on radio talk shows nationwide. It wasn't the nanny who was to blame, cried the right wing of motherhood, it was the mother's fault for working and not being home with her baby. Yet this same contingent would have welfare mothers get off the dole by getting a job, regardless of whether that means leaving their kids in suboptimal child care in order to do so. What'll it be, it is tempting to ask, work or motherhood?

The answer, ultimately, is simpler for those who don't have to make the choice based strictly on their personal income. It is easy for women dependent on men with generous incomes to criticize other mothers for working—until the generous income dries up or the head of such a household takes off with his secretary. It's equally gratuitous for women without ambition to attack those whose personal motivations differ from theirs, or to see paid work as a morally corrupt self-indulgence and distinctly inferior to the same number of hours spent volunteering as a Junior Leaguer. This ideological divide has impeded women from making sensible choices that best fit their family's needs without being subject to criticism by other women who have chosen to configure things differently or just had different luck.

Men, interestingly, may drive the hope for reconciling this fractured sisterhood. Even though the numbers remain vanishingly small, more dads are taking turns staying home with the kids. (The operative words here are "taking turns," because rare is the dad who adopts domesticity as a long-term or permanent position or ambition.) As these fathers discover the joys of hands-on parenting, they apply the business model to being at-home dads, seemingly unable to resist doing what they've done for years, perhaps because old habits die hard.

While women coming into the business world initially stepped right into men's shoes, went to men's conventions, and measured themselves by men's standards, the fellas have learned well by watching these mistakes. In stepping into women's roles, husbands are determined to keep wearing their own shoes. At-home dads have lost no time putting out niche newsletters, setting up Web sites, writing books about the experience (sometimes they stay home just long enough to write the book, then get back to "real" work), and even setting up dad-run daycare centers. And because any good career deserves a convention, the second annual At-Home Dad's Convention was held in Chicago in 1997.

If we can take this as a good sign and resist the temptation to notice too audibly that women have not only been doing these at-home things for centuries but have been welcoming men to join them at it for at least that long, then we will be on our way to shared understandings heretofore unfathomable. Within the context of a family, taking on domestic respon-sibilities at the expense of a career or job requires that a person reevaluate his or her sense of independence. Taking the complementary route and going out the door to work every day also demands relying on someone else, this time to caretake the domestic necessities. How well a couple lives with these issues of mutual dependency can make or break a marriage, yet striking a workable balance can be tricky.

Women who have been raised and educated to fend for themselves, who have paid their own rent and sometimes tuition, and who have made their own financial and lifestyle decisions for a decade or so before mar-rying may have a difficult time adjusting to being unemployed—gainfully speaking. Financial dependence on a spouse can make someone in this sit-uation feel like a kept woman, regardless of how tirelessly she works on behalf of her family. The absence of a paycheck, community property laws notwithstanding, can create the sensation of a lopsided dependency.

Because my entire young adulthood was spent providing for myself, I still hate drawing on my husband's professional account for a deposit to our household account. And even on days that begin by driving my daughter to her swim workout at 5:30 A.M. and go nonstop until I'm doing the last of the dinner dishes at 11:00 P.M., I may feel as though I haven't done my "share" because there's no paycheck involved. Fortunately, on an intellec-tual level, I'm quite clear about the real—if unpaid—value of my contri-bution to our family on days like this.

Men, on the other hand, generally have an easier time with the sort of dependency required of them as breadwinners. The majority of men are raised to depend on mothers, female housekeepers, or sisters to cook, clean, do laundry, and care for children. Having wives perform these tasks is not only an extension of what they are already accustomed to, but also doesn't pose a threat to their sense of power or independence. In many instances, it's probably pretty convenient if not downright expected, with some men feeling entitled to being taken care of because they bring home the money. No wonder women feel disproportionately dependent.

Perhaps when men's numbers on the domestic front begin to approach those of women, the picture of mutual dependency will come into balance. Nonetheless, domestic labor is not likely to be placed on a par with paid labor any time in the foreseeable future. Apart from dislocating long-standing traditions within religious and personal contexts, the political ramifications of this sort of rearrangement foreclose any such imminent possibility. Such things take generations, at least, to reorder.

Even if the impossible were attempted, and monetary values could be assigned to domestic labor, the delineations between men's work and women's work would persist. That the state of Alaska was willing to contemplate allowing subsistence hunting to take the place of paid work in allocating welfare eligibility says it all. Hunting, after all, is manly work. If woman's work was given the same status, welfare moms wouldn't have to leave their kids to get work because each one could honestly say they already had a job.

It remains, then, for mothers—and fathers—to give themselves ample credit for the work they perform at home. Someday, maybe even before the slowly growing population of men who are willing to take on womanly work has reached a critical mass, mothers and fathers may be able to look to another version of the GDP, one that tells the real story of work. Until then, raising a family and keeping a home will continue to be a tough, satisfying, but unpaid job, and someone with the savvy to recognize its worth will have to keep on doing it.

Run the Numbers

If a sociological picture could be stitched depicting how professional women with children patch together solutions to keeping family and soul together, it would look more like a crazy quilt than any well-thought-out or deliberate pattern. A quaint little Schoolhouse, a carefully measured Grandmother's Fan, or a tidy Log Cabin design, it is not. A friend who works as a book publicist and mothers one son remarked once that she was sure the cultural developments over the past thirty years were a premeditated conspiracy to drive women crazy. Although she said this half jokingly, it was with an underlying tone of genuine desperation and conviction. Having been drawn toward a career she loved without any preparation for what would happen when she became a mother, she felt that despite being very good at what she does professionally, she had been set up to be frustrated. This is a common theme among mothers who are also professionals.

Not the least of the cumulative and chronic frustrations inherent in the work-family dilemma is the way money flows into a number of sinks. Even if the emotional pieces involved in finding and keeping good child care could be put aside, and even for some of those most successful in their fields, the overhead that has to be paid in order to walk out the door to work each day remains an issue. After deducting taxes, the cost of doing business for any mother includes paying for surrogate care and probably some housekeeping. And while prospective estimates may see these as minimal financial considerations, they always take a bigger chunk of what was once disposable income than anyone ever imagines in advance.

Another friend, a woman who graduated from one of the Ivy League schools with a degree in engineering and received her Ph.D. in the same field, is a case in point. After working at a university for several years, through the births of her first four children, she had an eye-opening consultation with her accountant when she was pregnant with her fifth child. They determined that by the time she paid taxes, then paid a baby-sitter and a housekeeper in after-tax dollars so she could go to work, she was looking at a financially losing proposition. If she was going to support a "hobby," as she put it, there were other things she'd rather be doing.

I recall feeling the same way when, after my second was born, I began working about twenty hours a week in an urgent-care clinic. By the time I paid federal, state, and local taxes; a self-employment tax; a baby-sitter to care for the baby; a private Montessori school to educate my four-year-old; and our housekeeper to provide consistency throughout the comings and goings of nannies, I had enough money left over to buy a bag of groceries each week. That I was contributing in any meaningful way to the basics of food, shelter, transportation, and clothing for our family was an illusion or delusion, depending on how I looked at it. It took me a while to realize that twenty hours of my time is an awfully steep price for a bag of groceries. There is no way around this circumstance: gainfully employed mothers of young children, regardless of their socioeconomic standing or job, either pay to replace themselves at home or end up doing double duty. The latter invariably has its own price, albeit one that doesn't show up on any balance sheet or paycheck.

In an effort to minimize these financial hits, families often arrange for live-in help, since providing room and board usually means more bang for the cold-cash bucks. For some families, particularly those who can offer separate accommodations, this arrangement works well. For others, it's a little like adopting a teenager when you are still trying to figure out a toddler. Instead of having a few manageable sources of stress as you walk out the door each day, you now have—most parents of teenagers do—stressors you never dreamed of and can't begin to determine how to address.

Yet the expectations with which women in my age cohort were raised can make it difficult to separate one cause of stress from another. You are more likely to blame a horny husband, an incompatible boss, an inadequately trained preschool teacher, a lazy housekeeper, and, of course, the baby-sitter for putting obstacles in your way than to see the collective picture for what it is, something other than what you spent all those years counting on. So thoroughly did women buy into the expectations of having their own money to spend and of earning money that would make their lives more comfortable rather than less, that it can take a long time to come to terms with where the money really goes.

For some women—depending on other sources of family income, number of children, and personal psychology—the income they derive from work makes life more comfortable and affords their children with necessities or enrichment that wouldn't otherwise be possible. For other women, the sense of satisfaction and self-esteem they gain from work justifies the overhead, counterbalances any stress generated by having to juggle, and makes them better moms. For still others, like my friend the engineer, the demands of motherhood will periodically negate the impact of any income or satisfaction derived from working. And while certain of these scenarios may make the work-family dilemma seem like a nefarious conspiracy or a setup for frustration, it's really just a patch on the unique crazy quilt of a mother's life, a patch that often needs to be stitched, undone, and restitched before it fits with the rest of the many patches.

Plan for the Educational Freight

Families confront a multitude of social problems today that weren't around, at least at their current magnitudes, thirty years ago. That these social problems inevitably come with a personal price tag has exacerbated the difficulties facing families today. Preeminent among these social ills, one that generates considerable emotional and financial anxiety for families across class lines, is the deterioration of public education. And while it's tempting to weep, wail, gnash teeth, and retreat into the position that life isn't fair, this won't fix the problem or get your children educated.

When I was in college in the mid-1970s, the tuition at the privately funded school I attended was about $3,000 a year; today it costs more than that to attend many "free" state-funded universities. During the early 1980s, the annual tuition at George Washington Medical School was an astounding $12,000; today this is a fraction of the prices at private colleges. Just the cost of sending a child to a private preschool nowadays is upward of $5,000 a year, while tuitions for private elementary educations run in the neighborhood of $7,000 to $10,000 a year. The dilemma was summed up well by humor-columnist Dave Barry when he wrote, "We parents must encourage our children to become educated, so they can get into a good college that we cannot afford."

The education quandary begins very early in parenthood and is of a dimension that can catch a couple off guard. Two types of programs exist for preschoolers: day care and early childhood education. Better and worse examples of these can be found in each category, with the price tags typically reflecting the quality; in educational circles, the dictum "You get what you pay for" holds up. Another variable besides price is the age range a school or daycare center is licensed to handle. Because increasing evidence points to the first three years of a child's life as providing a crucial groundwork for everything that comes later, many daycare centers are adopting the materials and techniques of early childhood-education programs. And while this is generally a favorable development for children, it can be a financial burden for parents who will almost always find that the younger the child and the more educational the program, the higher the price.

Parents often agonize over whether to leave their infant or toddler in any type of group setting, be it educational or not. Most of us have no family history or personal experience on which to base this decision and, of course, expert advice runs the gamut from yes to no. This is one more decision that will depend on personal considerations including your financial situation, your child's temperament and health, the availability of a good group setting, and the necessity for surrogate care.

From a medical viewpoint, placing infants in group care has its distinct disadvantages. An infant's developmental task is to stay healthy and establish a trusting relationship with his caregivers. The greater the number of caregivers, the more confusion and exposure to illness will factor into a child's situation. And because childcare personnel tend to have not only a high absentee rate but a high turnover, the consistency on which preschoolers—especially infants—thrive can be hard to come by. As a result, and because predictability, safety, and health are the primary considerations early on, the best type of surrogate care for infants is usually provided in very small and personal group settings or by a good baby-sitter who comes to the home.

If it is affordable and the caregiver is loving and imaginative, this arrangement can be ideal for a long time. Sometime around the age of eighteen months, however, aided and abetted by their ability to walk and increasingly communicate, toddlers become more outgoing and begin to follow their relentless curiosity further and further. For many children, this is a good time to introduce them to a group educational setting for several hours a day so they can explore new materials, begin to socialize with other children, and learn to trust that their parents or caregiver will return. The inevitable downside to any group arrangement right up through kindergarten is the fact that it facilitates the spread of infectious disease, and for this reason, children who are susceptible to recurrent ear and respiratory infections should avoid group settings until they are older.

Preschool, however, is only the tip of the iceberg when it comes to educational costs. When a child is old enough to attend elementary school, the choice of venue and price varies even more than at the preschool level, but once again, the decisions are not always simple. When our oldest daughter was not yet one year old, my husband and I bought a home in what, at the time, was one of the better public school districts in our area. Four years later, when she was ready for kindergarten, the school was no longer as clearly desirable as it had seemed when we began paying our mortgage. Whether this was more apparent than real was hard to say; our perspectives had been altered by the high standards of the preschool we had chosen, and this constituted our only experience with formal education for our child. The public school, which some people still held in high regard, looked dowdy, disorganized, and crowded when compared to what we were used to. We were accustomed to having two well-trained, experienced teachers for every twenty-four students, not the one-to-thirty ratio we saw in the public school. Besides these basic differences, the public school abided by inflexible policies about classroom assignments and had nonnegotiable rules and regulations on many other counts. And while all this combined to make us feel we had been spoiled by the high quality of private school education, we didn't feel the least bit spoiled by the high price of the option we chose.

What was curious to me as I became more educated about education, was that in actual dollars allocated per student enrolled, the public schools compared quite similarly to the private schools. At one point, when we were paying $5,400 in annual private school tuition, the school voucher issue became an election issue in our state. During the debate, it was repeatedly cited that the number of dollars the state supplied per student to each public school district was $5,200. Yet for a couple of hundred dollars a year more, my kids were getting, in addition to the requisite academic instruction, classes in French, music, drama, and art. Public school apologists would say that private schools, by virtue of selective admissions criteria, didn't have to contend with problem students and therefore had more resources to allocate to everyone else. Our Montessori school, however, was frequently viewed as and used as a setting where kids who were having problems in the public schools would thrive. Ultimately, the difference in cost-effectiveness between public and private schools is impressive and doesn't inspire faith that other aspects of the public educational process are going to be handled any more wisely.

Most of this discussion is moot for families living in good—which usually means affluent—public school districts, where elementary education can be obtained at little or no out-of-pocket cost. Still, the time cost of staying actively involved in a school's PTA and being available to volunteer for various activities remains. Parent involvement is so crucial to the well-being of any school, whether public or private, that many private schools with high tuitions also require a minimum number of volunteer hours from each family.

The need and purpose of parent participation may be more apparent to a mother than to a father, as was illustrated by a conversation I overheard one day in which a woman was describing to her husband the various areas in their kids' school that needed parents to volunteer. The father, without giving the matter much consideration, declared that both he and his wife were too busy working and doing what was necessary at home to think about volunteering. According to him, it was time they just couldn't afford. His wife, being closer to the day-to-day workings of the school, replied that being actively involved with their children's school wasn't something they could afford not to do. The importance of maintaining some kind of volunteer presence at a child's school doesn't change, and indeed may become more important, as kids get older. Junior high and high school can be the time you most need to keep your finger on the pulse of your child's educational experience.

Junior high and high school, however, often seem as remote as Social Security benefits to new parents with young children. Still, if low-cost educational options are suboptimal and a couple is spending their retirement savings on their kids' preschool and elementary educations, sooner or later they're bound to wonder which age benefits most from this expense. I hear this question pondered regularly as parents transfer kids to public elementary schools, citing the need to conserve their funds for junior high, high school, or college. I've wondered about this myself, knowing that the money I have spent on private school tuition over the years has been at the expense of other experiences and may ultimately compromise the dollars available for college tuitions. As I've watched my four children wend their way through various school scenarios, I've sometimes felt as though I'm conducting an experiment in educational outcomes with my home as the laboratory. If I were asked to reach a conclusion based on data accumulated to date, I'd point to the early years as the critical piece in the educational puzzle.

This conclusion—that loading the front end of a kid's education with whatever resources are available is the way to go—stems from several observations. One has to do with having started my first three kids in a Montessori toddler program when they were each about eighteen months old. When my fourth child, Francesca, reached the same age, not only were we already paying three tuitions, but I had markedly curtailed my work hours to meet family needs, which meant I had more time than money. I organized a group of five mothers with children the same age as my youngest, and each mom took one day of the week to spend several hours educating the group. Although this system worked well for several years from a convenience standpoint, and although the kids were well socialized, when my daughter began Montessori school at age five, she spent the first two or three years catching up in math and reading readiness with her peers who had been through preschool. This was one reality check about the value of starting formal education early.

Another check came when, after my older children finished sixth grade at their Montessori school, they switched to the public junior high and eventually the public high school. I worried endlessly about this transition. Should I have saved the tuition for the treacherous teen years; would they make friends or would they feel isolated when they most needed to feel connected; would they be able to handle the change in teaching methods; would they fall through the cracks in such a big place; would they go into culture shock? When no such disasters befell them, and when the soundness of their educational background and love of learning translated into straight A's, I worried that they were not being sufficiently challenged. Finally it dawned on me that being challenged didn't mean they had to struggle in high school any more than they did in grade school. Because formal education has been a way of life for them since before they can remember, each educational step is just a logical, comfortable, and expected extension of the steps that went before. Fostering this eagerness to learn from a very young age makes great sense.

Compute the Big Picture

The high cost of activities that were once taken for granted leads to wishful thinking. In conversations about everything from schools to summer camps to organized sports, one parent sooner or later says to another, "It never used to be like this. What's wrong with the way things were? After all, it was good enough for me when I was a kid." Yet what was good enough for kids thirty or forty years ago was good enough in a very different context. Times have changed dramatically for families.

During the sixties and seventies, children (today's parents) stayed home, usually with their mothers, until they were old enough to attend kindergarten. After this they went off to schools where the biggest safety issue revolved around the playground bully, who may have thrown fists but didn't fire off rounds. Schools may have been repressive, but they were well funded and not, for the most part, consumed with the task of addressing social problems at the expense of class time.

After school, kids returned to neighborhoods where an adult was present in most homes, after-school sports consisted of stick ball in an empty lot or roller skating on the block, and dinner was served at six. Families spent evenings together, doing homework or watching television. The details of day-to-day household care like laundry, cleaning, and shopping had been taken care of during the day by the parent who stayed home and didn't fracture family time right up until bedtime. Weekends were reserved for family recreation, gardening, entertaining, worship, and household repairs. A reasonable rhythm prevailed.

Everything is different now. Where families once revolved around parents and children, they now revolve around schedules and finances. Mom and Dad both have demanding calendars, but so too does each child, right down to the baby. Mom goes to work in one direction and Dad in another. The baby goes to day care, the toddler to preschool, and the older kids to various grade schools. These older children often return home to empty homes and neighborhoods, then watch television until an adult returns and dinner can be hustled together or pizza delivered. The evenings are short on relaxation and long on things that have to get done before bedtime. Weekends are dissipated by playing catch-up, working second jobs, or succumbing to plain old fatigue. The old reasonable rhythm is notably absent.

A whole new pace and direction is in place. Adults have become slaves to tightly organized lives and have, in order to know where their children are at all times, penciled the kids into planned activities and organized sports where unsupervised play once reigned. Gone are sleepy mornings and family breakfasts, displaced by mad dashes and before-school child care. Gone is year-round sandlot baseball; here to stay are sports for every season with after-school practices. And gone are luxurious, unplanned summer days, replaced by serial day camps that double as child care.

This need to fill in the blanks that once speckled childhood with spontaneous time to imagine, create, daydream, play, and read is a mixed bag. Such planning keeps kids busy and provides learning opportunities that might not otherwise be present, which at a time when schools are cutting back on enrichment programs is not all bad. This busyness has, however, cost children their leisure and cost parents the money it takes to have other people constantly supervising their kids. Soccer, piano, golf, chess, art, drama, and tutoring keep kids going nonstop between bouts of school, sleep, homework, and television, and give the checkbook its daily workout.

Admittedly, all was not rose-colored in the past. Women were over-qualified for doing nothing but keeping house, catering to their spouse, and supervising kids. They were often bored, understimulated, and deeply unhappy. This discontent, which eventually took its toll on marriages, broke through the chin-up facade with force during the seventies when the divorce rate began to skyrocket. The reaction to not having enough to do, however, has been to go to the other extreme, haphazardly and without a good picture of how things would change.

As a result everyone, especially the kids, has become stuck without options. In pursuing life choices, many women have found themselves with fewer options than ever. Somewhere in the great space that exists between being exclusively domestic and working full-time plus handling all the domestic responsibilities lies a happy medium—not only for women, but for their work and parenting partners as well. This compromise may sound, considering it requires time away from gainful employment, like an alternative too expensive to explore. But for the family's soundness, the parents' happiness, and the children's well-being, we really can't afford not to strive for modified work-family arrangements more deliberately.

Expect the Unexpected and Budget for It

The story of how so many couples come to live from one round of bill paying to the next, and consequently from sleep to job to sleep with little or no leisure in between, could be told by their financial histories. How two people go from owing on a college loan or two when they start out, to acquiring a hefty mortgage, business loans, credit card debt, and a slew of monthly insurance, utility, tuition, and home personnel bills is as accurate a portrayal of a marriage as that available in any photo album. Early on, finances are like the smiling, romantically smitten duo on their honeymoon. Later, the extra pounds begin to figure into the photos in the album and the numbers in the ledgers. This extra weight is difficult to carry.

There is, particularly for couples who can't communicate well about money or have different spending philosophies, an insidious process that often begins with the obvious and obscure expenses for the first child. The hospital and doctor bills not covered by insurance, the childcare costs, the bills for baby equipment, nursery furniture, and new clothes for Mom— all hit within a short time interval. "Whew," the happy but broke couple think. "We're glad that's over so our finances can get back to normal." But, of course, it's all just beginning.

Soon there's another kid. Now the house is too small, and, if the romance is still in a marriage, the new house, an icon of boundless optimism, is sure to be a fixer. Though the excited couple is certain the necessary repairs will pay off in the long run—and they may—the house, in the meantime, is a bottomless money pit. This doesn't matter, however, because even homes in top condition become money sinks eventually, and sooner when kids live in them. Laundry appliances don't do well when golf tees get into the motors, plumbing resists having large items forced into small pipes, paint chips when kicked, carpeting becomes irretrievably worn and stained when constantly deluged by food, floors rot when bathtubs continually overflow, windows give way to baseballs, cabinet hinges bend under the weight of a child riding the door, and towel bars don't hold up as gymnasium equipment. (This damage doesn't take long to accrue. Every time we've rented a vacation house for a couple of weeks, the security deposit has been forfeited. One time there were tire marks on the wooden deck where my four-year-old taught herself to ride a bike. Another time a painter had to be paid to remove the ball marks from the ceiling in the kids' bedroom.) After keeping up with repairs for some time, the couple will almost certainly want to go several financial steps further and undertake a kitchen remodel.

The house, nonetheless, is only one money drain. The car that served nicely for one-person commutes to work before kids arrived is inevitably too small, too old, or not safe enough once a small passenger or two or three is on board. Before long, the first child needs braces, the younger one is in preschool, and a third is a different gender than the first two and needs a wardrobe all his own. Mom and Dad do the only thing they can think to do and apply for a fourth credit card because the mortgage and other three credit cards are maxed out.

Each additional child will take a toll on the household budget just as he will on his parents' time. Kids are not, as is wishfully thought, cheaper by the dozen. Scheduling family life means that ideally each and every child would come with his or her own monthly coupon booklet. Where mothers once said to groups of kids, "Go play," they now stop on their way home from work to pick up one child from a piano lesson, another child from an art class, and a third from the golf course. The low-budget group rate represented by "Go play" has been raised enormously by the need to keep track of who goes where when both parents are otherwise occupied. Even for siblings who both or all attend the same after-school child care or summer camp, the fees are individual. If you're lucky there might be a 10 percent sibling discount.

Historically, children have been added to families by dint of whims. It is only after the fact that the realities of what each individual child adds to the family hits home. The bigger the family the bigger the income needed to support it because big families need big cars and big houses and have big grocery and clothing bills. The bigger the income needed, the more time Dad and Mom have to spend making money. The more time Dad and Mom spend making money, the more money they have to pay other people to do things for them and to watch their children. In the worst cases, you have to look harder and harder in the midst of a chaotic existence to see the family at all.

As all these expenses seep into a family's yearly accounting like rainwater into the poorly designed sunken garage, the couple keeps working harder and harder to stay ahead of the tax man and maintain the lifestyle to which they have become accustomed. Even the couple who has stashed a nest egg, been in on the stock market's climb, or has a modest trust fund from which to draw can find themselves pinched. Yet retreating from a habitual level of spending is not only extremely difficult and often too little too late, but when necessary, has to happen vis-à-vis monthly costs that never seem to level out. Testifying to this is the number of personal bankruptcies that rose markedly during the mid to late 1990s, despite the robust economy.

Of course, the situation is not so dire for everyone. Lots of couples start out with jobs, then get promotions and pay hikes commensurate with their ever-increasing home expenses. Other couples follow sequential five-year plans that actually go according to schedule. Some fortunate duos have been clairvoyant about the stock market, and some couples even save for their retirements and stay within a monthly budget. This last, in the absence of other sources of income, is the only certain way to keep pace with the gradual accumulation of expenses that will come to pass, whether it is planned for or not.

For many families, my own included, life seems like a never-ending game of financial catch-up. Just when I think the last bill has been paid and we're finally in a break-even position, the water heater leaks, taxes are more than estimated, the car needs a new transmission, or one of the kids needs speech therapy and orthodontia. I could solve all of this by spending more time in an office setting, but while this would create greater financial comfort, the trade-off would be less emotional comfort, not only for me but for the whole family.

Ultimately every family has to establish its own set of priorities and make decisions based on income and an individual sense of what's important. In my home, a complicated and ever-changing balance is struck between home expenses, education, kids' activities, travel, entertainment, and how much work my husband and I can do. Neither of us have ever been to Hawaii, my husband's never been to Europe, and our family vacations are limited to places we can reach by car. Our individual call has been to make the financial stretch to keep the kids in Montessori schools and forego vacations. And, of course, the discussion about all these decisions and compromises is an ongoing one.

Having said all this, another pitfall bears mentioning. Some couples tread so carefully and are so averse to taking any risks that by the time they go after the home in which they hoped to raise their family, the kids, dog, cat, goldfish, and hamster are gone. When children are very small, they don't care if they have their own room, Corian counters in the kitchen, or the latest in video and sound equipment. Teenagers, on the other hand, care deeply about privacy and appearances. Sometime between infancy and adolescence, children commit to eternal memory a sense of their upbringing, into which a number of things will factor: comfort, safety, aesthetics, interpersonal relationships, humor, and educational inspiration. How the family budget is allocated will color a child's memory to some degree. The final picture will be one that no camera can take, but that a child's heart will hold in its album forever.

Chapter Seven

Just When You Think
It's Going to Get Easier,
It Won't

It's always something.
—Gilda Radner

Preeminent among the many myths that pave the road to the work-family dilemma is the notion that as children get older, things become easier and life gets back to "normal." In reality, the opposite supposition is closer to the truth. The elementary years don't abide surrogate care as smoothly as does the preschool era, and teens require large amounts of parental attention, presence, and affection. Moreover, as children get older they travel in ever-widening circles, making the logistics of parenting more complicated than when the kids' activities revolved around home or preschool. Flexible schedules are at a premium during these years, as are collaborative arrangements between parents. Despite a tendency to be time-pressed and challenging, this time can also be the most gratifying of all the child-rearing years for the parent who is on hand to enjoy it.

Enjoy the Good Old Days Now

Parenting wizards have given us more information that we can use about pregnancy and the first month, year, and five years of a child's life. Anyone who has ever been a parent is intimately familiar with expert wisdom on spit up, crawling, first steps, car seats, sleep disturbances, breast pumps, diaper rash, temper tantrums, nightmare nannies, bottle mouth, and all the other war stories and developmental details of raising infants, toddlers, and preschoolers. Once kindergarten begins, however, you're pretty much on your own.

The tendency of helpful parenting information to dwindle to a trickle when advising about children past the age of five or six is due to a couple of phenomena. By the time parents have traversed the prekindergarten stage, they have usually come to terms with the notion that parenting is a messy business and only peripherally amenable to expert advice. Editors of parenting magazines know this and target their marketing efforts at the ever-emerging supply of new parents rather than at experienced parents, who after a few years become disillusioned with superficial or quick-fix parenting solutions.

The other reason the market for how-to parenting info is skewed so heavily toward the early years is that we've tried to convince ourselves that the labor-intensive years of child raising lighten up substantially when school kicks in. So certain is the notion that life begins to resume a modicum of normalcy when kids begin school that we call the years from age six until adolescence "latency," implying a dormant period for kids and, we are quick to imagine, a concomitant renaissance for parents. This, however, may be the biggest child-rearing myth of all.

This false belief takes its strength from a number of proponents. The self-appointed moralists in our midst are righteously energized when they are protecting young children from misguided mothers who work away from home. These proscriptions against working, however, are mostly aimed at the years when children are young and ease up, becoming latent themselves, once kids are old enough for school. Perhaps because school is legally mandated, it behooves even the mightiest of moralists to relax enough to send their children out of the house for several hours a day. Perhaps too, even moral spokeswomen need a break after a while. Whatever the reason, age six is seen as the demarcation between needing Mom around full-time and being all right without her for five or six hours each day.

Another population that feeds the focus on the early years is professional mothers who, for a variety of reasons, decide to stay at home with their little ones. These women, accustomed to being productive in non-domestic spheres and taken aback by the intensity of the work-family dilemma, sit at their word processors during nap times and document the ups and downs of dedicated motherhood. This introspection has resulted in a tremendous lore that has examined motherhood from every possible angle. Although most of these chroniclers plan on returning to their profession, the naps eventually phase out and we never get to hear the continuation of the story—not, at least, in the rich detail that characterizes the first part. We are left thinking that the plot may only be as thick as taking care of one or two small children, and that when they are old enough for school, "normalcy" once again supervenes. If the truth be told, however, everything just gets so busy that introspective interludes at the computer become few and far between.

Further contributing to the notion that women get their lives back when kids board a school bus is plain old wishful thinking. Wouldn't it be nice—those of us who spent a bundle of time and money getting positioned to have it all tell ourselves—if all the expectations we had about being able to work and have families finally came to pass, even if they didn't materialize in the face of wee ones underfoot. It sounds so sane to have the kids occupied for half the day that we fall for yet another illusion.

The now familiar sequence of events that women of my generation discovered over time after having a baby, and that was documented so thoroughly by journal-keeping mothers of all stripes, went from trying to do it all and floundering to trying to do some of everything with varying degrees of success. With two or more children, however, even attempting some of everything became tricky; newborns showed up and threw a wrench in the expectation that work as we once knew it would resume when the firstborn went to school. It became, as children appeared sequentially and despite all our hopes, difficult to move any appreciable distance from square one.

The first part of this actuality was not the biggest surprise. Somehow, the unpredictability that came with babies made sense, even if we hadn't anticipated it. Of course infants woke up in the middle of the night and wanted to nurse; of course a toddler with a fever sidelined our other plans; of course we needed the afternoon off for the preschool parent-teacher conference. To accommodate these unexpected but reasonable reality roadblocks, we hired lots of help, went for a ride on the mommy track, or hunkered in at home with mashed bananas and board books to wait out toddlerhood. There was, after all, that light at the end of the tunnel called elementary school when our lives would settle down.

Little did we know how simple it all was then. Despite feeling over-whelmed from trying to put all the pieces of the child-rearing puzzle together, and without being aware of it, we were, nonetheless, in control of the essentials. Every morning we handed the kid or kids our agenda. "Here," we would say without understanding the simplicity of the ar-rangement. "Here is the baby-sitter," or, "Here is the preschool. Mommy will be gone for whatever amount of time she needs to be gone and will be back when she feels it's time to come back." The kids may have protested a little now and then, but this rarely stopped the forward motion of our daily plans. These small children made small demands on our time.

Just when we had gone the preschool and early elementary distance and were ready to get back to a more comprehensive work schedule, the hardy little folks we had nurtured toward greater autonomy developed agendas of their own. "Here," they said to us without a trace of manipu-lation or premeditation. "Here is what I'll be needing from you in the way of time and attention each day. Oh, by the way, here's why I don't want to play soccer or go to after-school child care or play with the kid next door—even though it works so well for your schedule. And one more thing, Mom: the main player has to be you or Dad, because now that the issues are more complicated than whether I get my diaper changed every hour or have the sand emptied out of my shoes before a nap, baby-sitters don't cut it anymore. I mean, what do I care if the baby-sitter watches my flag football game?" Latency, it suddenly became glaringly apparent, wasn't so latent after all.

Know Your Child Development Stuff

Every year in November, the upper elementary teachers in my children's school hold parent-teacher conferences for two full days. During this time, the children—fourth, fifth, and six graders—are expected to do volunteer work, preferably but not necessarily for a good cause. The main idea behind the program is to instill a commitment to community service at a young age, and while the concept is lovely, the success of the endeavor ultimately depends on how willing each set of parents is to come up with an appropriate situation for their child. Some of the kids tag along with one of their parents for a nonmedia take-your-kid-to-work day. Others find willing proprietors—of baseball card shops, coffee houses, daycare centers, newspapers, or just about any other organization where their parents have connections—to supervise them for several hours both days. Some children actually spend time working at one or another charitable organization.

For many years I did what most other parents did when faced with figuring out how to occupy a child for two days just a month before the winter holiday recess: I went into denial until the last minute. Consequently my kids have done make-work at the local zoo, dusted shelves in a store, and sorted golf balls at the nearby golf course. Once my daughter actually joined a group in a soup kitchen. Using the term "community service" loosely, my kids got by.

In October of the year my son was in fifth grade, he began the requisite reminders that the community service days were approaching. Finally, less than a week before the appointed days, in the face of the fifteenth prompting on the subject, I cast caution to the wind and suggested to my son that both of us stay home for at least one of the days and bake pies for a homeless shelter in town. I knew, as soon as I said it, that it would be a great experience for my son and put me hopelessly behind in my work schedule. Push-pull, pull-push.

My son loved the idea and rounded up a buddy whose mother had also put off figuring out how her son would fulfill his community service requirement. The three of us donned aprons the first morning and spent the day covered in flour, rolling out crusts, stepping around wayward apple peels, and mixing fillings. When we were done, the boys proudly counted four pumpkin, three apple crumb, and two pecan pies.

Our final task was to deliver the pies to the shelter which, I had determined in advance, fed about fifty-five men, women, and children—mostly families down on their luck—each evening. After we lined up the fruits of our labor on the stainless steel counter in the shelter's kitchen, one of the volunteer supervisors gave the boys a tour of the facility while expounding about the causes of and remedies for homelessness. The boys came away wide-eyed, talking nonstop about the full-on dinner they were going to do the following year and how else they might be able to help the homeless. More than just the immediate mission was accomplished.

This experience is just one of a jillion similar episodes that parents of school-age children face all the time. Because it is during this time that conscience formation is consolidated, socialization skills and peer interactions developed, and sexual behavior pondered and sometimes explored, the term "latency"—corresponding to the elementary school years—is misleading.

It is postulated that the oral, anal, and Oedipal upheavals of the earlier years are done, and the teen tasks lie way off in the future. And it is true that parents and teachers don't ask too much, a child is no longer a moment-to-moment danger to himself, and the balance of responsibility and fun weighs in favor of the latter. The world of the written word is discovered and life is good. Still, this is only a small part of the story of the elementary years.

During these years, kids spend many hours each day with adults and children outside their own families and are exposed to an array of values, religious beliefs, and worldviews other than those held in their homes. Ideally, a child's touchstone for processing his daily experiences and interpreting the various outlooks will be a thoughtful, concerned, and involved set of parents.

Many factors, however, get in the way of an optimal parent-child interaction at this time. The social milieu hurries children into adulthood, rendering the concept of latency obsolete for many kids. Television, movies, and print media present a proliferation of images and ideas, throwing adult realities into the face of younger and younger audiences, while at the same time, overextended parents are less and less available to monitor this exposure or discuss the resultant impressions. Many parents return to work or increase their work hours when children go to school, compounding the availability problem.

For many parents, the middle years of marriage—when children are elementary school-aged—are typically characterized by hard work on the home, interpersonal, and career fronts. Many marriages don't make it this far, and the breaking up process often derails a child's educational focus and ability to sort out relationship rights and wrongs. Divorce impedes a child's access to certain parental counseling and, given joint custody arrangements, can be a logistical nightmare just when a child is trying to get organized. The elementary years are a time during which kids develop "heart," and though some divorces are decidedly better than others, no divorce is terribly kind to a child's heart.

Everyone is hurried, and hurried parents tend to hurry their children by expecting them to see the world through adult eyes. One of the saddest examples of this type of prematuring came when seven-year-old Jessica Dubroff's father, saying it was her idea, set his daughter up to try to break a flight record in 1996. On one leg of the journey, their plane got caught in a storm during takeoff and crashed, killing them both. Much was said in the national press about this father's motives, but one thing remained crystal clear: setting a flight record is nowhere on the developmental task agenda of a seven-year-old. The contrast between the intent of the adult and the child in this instance was particularly apparent in my home where my youngest, also seven years old at the time, was playing dress-up, dancing to kid music, procrastinating about practicing her piano, and giggling through her first error-studded softball game. She and every other seven-year-old child are entitled to having grownup pursuits—things like flying a plane—be nothing more than dress-up or backyard fantasies for many years to come.

Another telling trend in our hurry-up world is the search for ways to modify children's behavior. Twenty years ago, for instance, the terms "attention deficit disorder" (ADD) and "attention deficit hyperactivity disorder" (ADHD) were obscure psychological concepts. Now, if a speaker wants to fill an auditorium, she need only include ADD or ADHD in the talk's title and anxious parents who rarely take time out from their busy schedules to do anything else will line up hoping to hear answers. Nearly every medical journal that crosses my desk contains an article about these disorders.

ADHD is defined as a "persistent pattern of inattention and/or hyperactivity-impulsivity that is more frequent and severe than is typically

observed in individuals at a comparable level of development." By definition, ADHD is a subjective diagnosis and not a testable medical or psychological entity. Because of this, ADHD remains in the interpretational realm.

There is no question that some children have poorer impulse control
and ability to focus for periods of time than others. There is also no question that a percentage of these kids experience dramatic improvement in
their ability to perform in school and various other situations when treated
with certain medications. But while pursuing medical avenues is worthwhile for a child struggling in school or with peer relationships, many kids
who won't respond to medication can be helped by other interventions
including speech therapy, sensory motor integration therapy, auditory
testing, vision assessments, or dietary modification. Lots of things that
look like ADHD are amenable to therapeutic interventions other than
drug therapy.

In addition to children who demonstrate a response to medication and
those with identifiable learning disabilities, a large group of children with
behavioral issues can benefit enormously from psychological counseling,
particularly family therapy. Very often it's not something intrinsic to the child
that results in problem behaviors, but something about the child's environment. A passage from Willa Cather's *My Antonia* (Houghton Mifflin, 1918),
in which Jim Burden describes Antonia's son, Leo, illustrates this:

> The boy was so restless that I had not had a chance to look at his face.
> . . . His mother said he got hurt oftener than all the others put together.
> He was always trying to ride the colts before they were broken, teasing
> the turkey gobbler, seeing how much red the bull would stand for, or
> how sharp the new axe was.

This, if ever there was one, is the description of a child who in most con-
temporary settings would be labeled with ADHD. Yet setting can be everything. Dr. Stanley Turecki, author of *The Difficult Child* (Bantam Books,
1985), makes this point by contrasting the situation of a young girl growing
up on a farm in Texas with several older brothers and lots of room to cavort,
with that of the same child being raised in a Manhattan apartment as an only
child with strict, older parents. The same behavior that looks normal on the
farm will look terribly problematic in the Manhattan apartment.

Adding interpersonal considerations to environmental factors further highlights behavioral problems. Marital discord in the home, such as a perfectionistic mother or an alcoholic father, may contribute to a child's inability to conform as surely as any genetic predisposition. And these phenomena come into play more acutely when parents are stressed by various factors, not the least of which are work-family time pressures. The combination of less time available at home to explore, bond, or work things through with parents and more time spent in structured environments with adults who have varying degrees of tolerance can add up to behavioral breakdowns. Children are experts at taking the temperature of their environments, but are much better at acting out their assessments than they are at articulating them calmly.

The elementary school years are a time for parents to stand at attention, be present, be involved, connect regularly, and shower their children with affection. Only then can a parent look at a child and say, at least for this one era of a child's life, mission conscientiously accomplished.

Don't Say No One Ever Told You

The labor-intensive, messy years of child rearing often correspond to the labor-intensive, mandatorily neat years of nurturing a career. Lots of women progress from grad school to marriage to babies in the course of developing their professional reputations. Having little ones at the breast or underfoot on the home front often seems the biggest obstacle to fast track or unfettered success on the work front. No wonder it's so tempting to believe that sending a child off to school will provide the ingredient necessary to pulling a work life out of a holding pattern and soaring to new heights.

Postponed childbearing and postponed gratification can combine, however, to change the direction of even most dedicated woman's drive. When motherhood occupies the same space on a time line as impending midlife, strange things can happen including new dramatic turns and changes of heart. The psychological fluidity that often intervenes at this time of a woman's life—from the late thirties to age fifty—can shed light on pathways and possibilities that may never before have been apparent or seemed imaginable. A woman who has longed for alternatives to the frantic pace, mad juggling, and attendant stress of balancing home and work may finally reach a turning point, when a now verbal child resoundingly requests her presence, and head toward personal equilibrium.

This is often instigated as much by sheer logistics as by any emotional X-ray vision. One day when my husband and I had four children ages seven and under, we were getting ready to go on a family picnic. An hour into the attempt to get everyone out the door, discouragement set in. "You know," I sighed, handing my husband one fully prepared child and reaching to change diaper number two, "this is probably as difficult as it gets. Not one of the kids is old enough to help with any of the others, and they're all so dependent on us for everything."

A few short years later I reconsidered my position. "You know," I said to my husband one day when our oldest was fifteen, our youngest seven, and I was heading to the car for my fifth drop off/pick up of the day, one of which had been to an out-of-town swim meet, "even if you remember it, forget what I said about little ones being the hardest. Four children, each with a sport or an instrument and none with a driver's license, that's got to be as time-intensive as parenting gets." Toddlers may be notorious for the power they wield over parents with potty training mishaps and tantrums, but at least their scenes can all take place close to home. Older children not only eat more, take up more physical and emotional space, argue more effectively, and get into more trouble than small kids, but they travel in ever-expanding circles—inevitably with a parent at the wheel.

Maybe it's the intensity with which we focus on a child's first few years of life that make us believe nothing could ever be more compelling. Perhaps it's children's vulnerability from a strictly physical standpoint that makes us attend to their infant and toddler needs so closely, and leads us to think that their increasing size and bulk will set us free. Yet even when we repeatedly see women retreat from career positions to be with school-aged kids, it always seems to take us by surprise. When Brenda Barnes left her high-level executive position at Pepsi in 1997, the news reverberated through national headlines for weeks. That she left at the top of her game while being groomed for a key executive spot and that she did so for personal reasons fascinated the business world no less than the world of mothers who had already gone that route. By way of explanation, she would say little more than that her kids didn't need to spend more time with her great support network, they needed more time with her.

Regardless of whether logistics, emotional intelligence, burnout, or midlife motivate the alteration of perspective, the net effect is the same. As children get older, women—and many men—tend to become increasingly invested in spending time with them. That most women still think differently until they are waist-deep in school-aged kids and that this is not a standard piece of lore handed down from one generation of mothers to the next is a curious phenomenon. The eventual truth is that the middle years of childhood require a more informed presence and attention than that demanded by babies. Inspiring this devotion is the certainty that no satisfaction in the world rivals that of seeing your kids do well in school, thrive emotionally, and excel athletically. Most often, however, what you see has a lot to do with what you've given.

Get It about Sibling Rivalry

It has been said that there are two kinds of families: those with one child and those with more than one child. In the former, a mother and father have the advantage of the parent-child ratio weighing in their favor. Communication factors, emotional dynamics, and things that can go wrong never get beyond a simple triangulation. With one child, Mom and Dad focus their hopes, dreams, time, energy, and money all in a single direction. Because this is quite a load of attention for any kid to contend with, day in and day out, there are distinct benefits to having both Mom and Dad at least somewhat preoccupied with work.

The biggest difference between families with one child and all other families is that more than one child begets competition for parental attention. All it takes is one sibling to transform the simple triangle into much more complicated geometry. While the first child is being toppled from his position at the center of the universe, his mother is realigning the strongest attachment she's ever experienced to include two children instead of one. Out of this upheaval emerges sibling rivalry. The pushes and pulls for parents to meet several needs at once, the wrenching intimacy of family bonds, and the petty jealousies that afflict human nature and revolve around parental attention, all come into play as soon as that second child arrives home.

I heard the best analogy I know, the one that gave me my first clue about the dimensions of sibling rivalry, shortly after my second child was born. Imagine a husband coming home one day and telling his wife that he is bringing home another woman but that he wants them to all live happily ever after. His wife has no say in this decision, nor is she able to leave. Her husband goes on to say, in a misguided effort to be understanding, that although this new woman is younger and cuter and will require most of his time, he wants his wife to know that he loves her just the same.

Each time a baby is added to a family, the older kids are put in the wife's position. Who can blame older siblings for saying things like, "Put the baby in the trash," or "Take the baby back to the hospital," when confronted with the tangible evidence that Mom and Dad will now have to be shared? Because of the discrepancy between the excruciating nature of this situation for both parents and children and the way it is publicly addressed, honest reactions from older children are frowned upon. These kids react by taking their feelings underground—though not so far that they can't access them vehemently when push comes to shove.

With each additional child, the old triangle becomes more remote and the interactive possibilities multiply. These are manageable when children are quite young, but become increasingly dicey as kids get older. Whereas a baby-sitter might easily distract a one-year-old from wanting his older brother's toy train, she might not be as effective when an eight-year-old, prompted by an older sibling's taunts, begins to throw fists.

I knew I had to reevaluate my work-to-home time ratio about the time my oldest was nine and her younger sister was six, when I came home from the office one day to find that the baby-sitter had taken them out to get slingshots. I'm not talking about anything flimsy, plastic, or the least bit safe; I'm talking about real heavy-duty metal wrist rockets. "They said you said they could have them," the sitter said in self-defense against my hanging jaw. Sibling rivalry, I saw in a moment of clarity, was the least of my worries. Sibling collaboration, despite being the goal of much of my mothering efforts, obviously needed to be watched closely.

When kids are small and cuddly and especially while they are still pre-verbal, surrogate care can take many forms. Indeed, lots of women embarking on working motherhood employ baby-sitters with scant command of the child's native tongue because what communicating gets done is all by sign language or intuition anyway. This changes dramatically when kids get older, and not only when it comes to communication. A whole host of questions needs to be addressed, requiring not simply good judgment but a deep, abiding, tangible knowledge of what makes a child tick, an ability that resides most competently with a particular child's parent.

As they come to that age—call it latency, the age of reason, or the age of logical thinking—when they begin to shape a more coherent world-view, a kindly teenaged or even middle-aged nanny is often in over her head. Children want clarification about religious issues and values, need their wounded feelings soothed, manipulate quite artfully, and know in no uncertain terms where the buck stops—and that it is rarely with a surrogate caregiver. It doesn't matter how competent a baby-sitter I hire; I'm still going to get that call on my cellular phone from my youngest complaining that her brother is drinking a soft drink that was supposed to be saved for a special occasion. In her mind, only Mom can definitively understand and enforce such tacit household rules.

Just as children can be the glue that holds two adults together over a long period of time, parents have to be the glue that holds kids together. To accomplish this, it is important to identify the factors that foster moments when siblings are, however temporarily, the best of friends. Figuring out which combination of kids and what situations, games, rituals, or team endeavors facilitate mutually good times for brothers and sisters will help create a cushion of benevolence and a store of good memories that children will call upon into adulthood.

Still, the indisputable fact is that siblings are rivalrous in the best of circumstances and in the most affectionate of families. And while they may love one another on some undetectable level, they may seem to hate each other on a much more ostensible, and for parents, uncomfortable one. Various factors often intensify the impact of this inescapable family reality, not the least of which is the number of children competing for a parent's attention and the availability of that attention. The less time and more children a parent has, the greater will be the inevitable discord. And, of course, the less time a parent has to spend with her family, the more entitled she will feel to having harmony abound whenever she is around.

When kids are little, an expectation for idyll may not be a big deal, and a parent won't expect a peaceful scene every time she walks in the door from work. She can, when faced with a gaggle of outstretched arms, sweep everyone onto the couch for a storybook or some other transition session. As kids get older, however, just herding everyone into one room is enough of a project without also trying to take their emotional or psychological temperature en masse. It becomes a more individualized process, more demanding, and, like it or not, a more time-consuming proposition to mother children as they increase in number.

Anticipate the Teens

Over the past century, our culture has transmogrified from one in which teenagers concentrated on their education, worked to help support the family, or, more likely, did both, to one in which teenagers are supported by their parents and are often left to their own devices. A number of trends have contributed to this change.

The economic necessity of making room in the job force for soldiers returning from World War II did more than just economically marginalize women; it did the same to the youth coming out of high school who might compete with returning GIs for a limited number of jobs. Continuing beyond a high school education thus became a better bet than hunting for jobs being saved for someone else. At the same time, the GI Bill provided funds for returning GIs who wanted to pursue or resume their education upon returning to America, an option that ultimately raised the marker on educational expectations all around. High-tech industry was also coming into its own, looking to employ those with educations beyond the high school level. Many teenagers who would have previously apprenticed themselves in a trade or gotten a jump on a career while still in high school no longer saw full-time employment as imminent and developed a more delayed approach to their futures.

Correspondingly, the postwar economy boomed. The standard of living edged upward, obviating the necessity of many teens to support themselves or contribute to their family's income. What money was earned in high school became disposable at a time when there was an expanding array of consumer items on which to spend it. Subsistence was out, consumerism was in, and teenagers had time and money like never before to do with as they chose.

Another factor that put teenagers in a category all their own was the rising expectation for longevity. A hundred years ago, the teen years comprised one-fifth or one-sixth of an individual's life, a sizable chunk and not to be taken lightly. The eight years from twelve to twenty now constitute about one-ninth or one-tenth of the long haul and have been relegated to a suspended animation of sorts, wherein little is expected from teenagers while much is demanded by them.

Over the past few decades, perhaps since the wholesale questioning of authority that occurred during the 1960s, other factors have conspired to make the teen years a treacherous demographic niche to occupy. The rise of the drug culture, the lifting of sexual taboos, a pervasive cultural preoccupation with deviance and violence, and, perhaps most important, the skyrocketing divorce rate have made it an exceptional feat to go the distance from age ten to twenty without getting tripped up by some adverse influence. The ubiquity of curious, bizarre, or self-destructive teenage behavior has made it not merely acceptable but commonplace for parents to publicly roll their eyes on the subject of their adolescent kids. It has also made parents chronically afraid for their teenaged children.

Not everything about teenhood is culturally determined, although many of its expressions certainly are. Japan's culture is often cited as being free from the same level of high-profile teenage rebellion that is witnessed in Western countries. Yet precisely the same hormonal and psychological factors that influence American teenhood influence Japanese teens. The difference has to do with the groundwork laid in the years preceding the teens and the expectations with which children grow up.

In Japan, a fairly homogeneous culture with a uniform set of values and expectations, there is sparse manifestation of teen turmoil. Not only are directions clear, but education, self-discipline, and conformity are universally and highly regarded. Teenagers in the United States, by contrast, are as diverse as the population. Socioeconomic status, religious and educational background, race, and regional identity all bear on what is expected of a child as she enters her teen years. Such influences notwith-standing, American teens face an enormous spectrum of choices and, per-haps understandably, may feel the only answers lie in experimentation with different possibilities.

The facts of psychology, the developmental tasks facing teens, are superimposed on these external factors. During these years a child seeks to establish her own identity, one separate from her parents. When parental supervision of the early and latent years has been repressive, a kid may have to be extra alternative, extra rebellious, or extra difficult to push her par-ents away and form a distinct self. Similarly, scant attention or free-for-all parenting may produce a confused, sad, flailing teen. Large wounds in family structure—as the result of a divorce, a parent's attention being redi-rected by remarriage, significant geographic dislocations during pre- or early adolescence, and poverty—can contribute to a teen out of control.

Even while they are working to free themselves from their parents, sib-lings, and past identifications, teens—more than ever before—need the consistency and stability of a home and parents who will love them no matter what they do. This doesn't mean that parents need to abide exces-sive rudeness, disruptive comings and goings, or illegal behavior. It does mean that power struggles will be ugly, that parental narcissism will hinder constructive outcomes, and that tolerance needs a large place in parent-teen interactions. In most cases, if the right stuff is in place from earlier years and has a continuity a child can expect, even the most testy teen will be amenable to reason, eventually.

The optimal arrangement for any human being, but perhaps especially for teens, balances responsibility with privilege. Because our culture has all but removed any expectations of responsibility from teenagers, while at the same time leaving all their privileges in place, a lopsidedness has devel-oped that is played out in counterproductive, often dangerous behaviors. The antidotes to this require parents' time and attention. Just because chil-dren are old enough to be left alone, appear able to fend nicely for them-selves, or can drive a car doesn't mean we can step back. It should come as no surprise to anyone that most teenage pregnancies get started between 3:30 and 6:30 in the afternoon, when homes are unsupervised and teens are idle. This time of a kid's life demands we be cautious all over again in new ways.

Although adolescents are eminently capable of holding a job or providing community service and desperately need the experience, it is unlikely that such work will ever be imposed on them. Yet a productivity void exists for teenagers and needs to be filled, righting their responsibility-privilege equilibrium. The task belongs to parents. This is where a sport, an instrument, a passion for art, or another extracurricular pursuit can make an enormous difference. Teens who regularly wear themselves out running, swimming, and competing in organized sports have just enough time to do their homework and sleep, which in their cut-loose world is good. Athletics have the added benefit of giving adolescent girls a pride and faith in their bodies that can at least partially neutralize the harmful societal messages about the purpose of the female body with which they are incessantly barraged. All these extracurricular involvements, however, are ultimately commitments for a parent as well as a child.

Another possible antidote to the twisting-in-the-wind teen syndrome is the availability of what author and child psychologist David Elkind calls "social capital" (*Parenting Your Teenager*, Ballantine Books, 1993). Having family, friends, and mentors—individuals with a child's history and best interests at heart—in the background to inspire adolescent energies in constructive ways and expect the best of a teen, steadying the ups and downs, is ever so important. Like all the other components of successful child rearing, however, these are best in place over the long haul, starting well before adolescence hits.

For my kids, social capital takes the form of their extended family. Holidays, birthdays, graduations, and other special occasions are always spent with some combination of aunts, uncles, cousins, grandparents, and friends. At Christmas time the adults each draw the name of one child and procure a special gift for that child. This has decreased the population of small dispensable toys and allowed each kid to get a substantial gift every year. My youngest sister, who has toddlers as my brother and I are negotiating the teen territory with our kids, recently suggested that the older teenagers be retired from this Christmas gift drawing to make room for the younger ones. That way, no adults would have to double up on gift buying as babies were added to the mix. I cringed when I read her e-mail suggesting this idea. As she will learn before long, teenagers, more than any of the other kids, need to be beholden to their adult relatives and to appreciate the generosity and attention of adults other than their parents. Only then will they feel the responsibility to give back by being individuals in which their whole family takes pride.

The concept of tough love has enjoyed a certain popularity of late. It is difficult for me to swallow the notion that, with teens, you fight fire with fire, especially since the teenager usually doesn't set, but inherits the fire. When applied to teens, tough love can be a heartbreaking solution to heartbreaking problems. And while there will always be the extremes of teen behavior, the real tough love needs to be what parents practice on themselves when their children are much younger. It is hard to sell things like self-discipline, postponed gratification, selflessness, fidelity, and dedication to parents, especially when the push of consumerism is to feel good, yet the importance of such rigors during the years when children are observing is absolutely crucial.

My guiding principle in dealing with my teenagers is humility. I sense strongly that, while I've worked hard to put the "right stuff" in place since they were born, anything can happen at any time and that the best place for me to be when it does is where they can reach me—not just by phone, but by heart. Nothing can be so bad, I've told them repeatedly, that you can't tell me, that together we can't figure out a good solution. But this first requires that they feel comfortable saying what's on their mind, and so the conversation around our house is often lively, if not always pleasant. It also means that I welcome their friends because if I didn't, they'd go somewhere else; I don't kid myself that I'm worth more to them than their friends. And finally humility means that I don't take things they say or do personally, even when those things are being yelled right at me. I try—I'm not always successful, but I try—to stay calm as a counterbalance to their intensity when things get dicey. I'm humble because the last thing they need to come up against at home is arrogance.

When kids are tiny, watching their firsts is a parental preoccupation. With camera in hand, a parent will dote on a toddler's every new move, every special occasion, every developmental landmark. That's the easy part. When those babies become teenagers, when they most need to be appreciated, reassured, and bolstered, the firsts don't seem so cute and sometimes don't even get recognized for the developmental landmarks they are.

Still, when they head out the door on their first date or get in a car with another teenager at the wheel, you want to be duly diligent, exercising a continuum of care that began way back when you strapped a toddler, now turned teenager, into a car seat. And when a kid calls later that night to ask if she can bring her friends home for a while, she should expect an "Of course." These are moments I wait for as distinctly as for all those baby firsts, supported by the knowledge that, one day and night at a time during the teen years, home is comfortable, friends are welcome, and, loud arguments and differences in perspective notwithstanding, all is well.

Know When to Hold and When to Fold

Saying you are going to communicate constructively with your partner and actually doing so are two different things. Very often the individuals comprising a couple feel they need to reach agreement about issues, even issues that don't have an impact on the nitty-gritty of their lives. They sense that if the other person "wins" a discussion, they automatically "lose." In many instances, however, being able to agree to disagree is the most useful and effective way to resolve a difference of opinion.

In certain situations, things are immensely simplified and facilitated when parents can strike an agreement about an issue before taking it up with their children. Most parenting books prescribe presenting kids with a united front so the kids aren't tempted to manipulate situations or pit parent against parent. But even so noble an undertaking as this can be tricky. The fact of the matter, in many instances, is that parents don't see eye to eye on things. Trying to convince children that you do agree is a form of dishonesty that may make kids more uncomfortable than the truth.

My kids, for example, know that their father would be happy to have a big-screen TV and spend more family time watching sporting events. They also know that their mother has kept her finger in this dike for years, pulling it out every so often to keep too much pressure from developing behind the wall, but closely regulating what and how much television gets through. The truce is, admittedly, an uneasy one, but one that has served its purpose for many years. In the long run I hope it will give my children some appropriate angst about watching television, that and lots of experiences they'd never have had if they had been watching the telly instead.

We live with two twenty-year-old television sets, no cable service, a broken set of rabbit ears, and one channel that gets fuzzy reception on a good day. I'm sure guests bite their tongues when they witness the scene in our family room and roll their eyes when they see my kids using a pair of scissors or a hemostat to turn on the TV or adjust the volume. The on-off knob was lost years ago when I removed it to prevent the kids from turning the set on at will. Since then I've tried screening out specific channels, making rules, and finally, canceling the cable service altogether. My husband used to say, "Get rid of the TV." The practical aspects of my having essentially taken him up on this, however, have long since worn thin. Now, he makes no secret, he wants more television time.

I, on the other hand, know what happens when the cable is restored, which it is occasionally for the World Cup, Olympic Games, or World Series. And because I am on the premises during the children's waking hours more often than my husband, I am the one who has to monitor four very creative kids and their never-ending reasons about why they should be allowed to watch TV. The problem, of course, is insidious. Just because one child has finished her homework, doesn't mean everyone else has. And just because everyone has finished their homework, doesn't mean the piano has been practiced. And just because everyone has finished everything else they are supposed to do, doesn't mean there aren't more thought-provoking ways to spend the rest of the evening, because, make no mistake, TV always involves the rest of the evening. Downtime takes a variety of forms, of which television is only one. The problem is that once the TV is turned on, by virtue of its seductive nature, it precludes all other options for that time.

The key piece in the ongoing debate about television in our house is that from a negotiating standpoint, my husband and I agree to disagree. From a practical standpoint, however, because I have to be the enforcer, the TV debate takes place on the stage of my preference. It's a little like keeping healthy, lower-fat foods on hand for the whole family even if only one person needs to watch his or her weight. The others are only going to benefit from the better diet. Similarly, keeping the whole family on a noncable diet isn't going to hurt any of them, even the ones who have the capacity to self-regulate the amount of TV they consume.

Parental collaboration, then, doesn't mean total or mindless agreement. Certain truces need to be established and revisited when the agreed-upon parameters break down. For instance, it is my opinion that corporal punishment—spanking or physical means of discipline—should not be negotiable. This is a subject that, because corporal punishment may enter each parent's disciplinary repertoire unintentionally, is easier for many couples to agree on than it is to put into practice. Most parents were spanked as children and, as a result, will spank a child out of anger or as a reflex rather than as a considered disciplinary option.

Having agreed with your spouse that neither of you will spank a child doesn't absolutely ensure that this will never happen. What the agreement provides, however, is an interventional platform, an entrée to the observing parent to step in when anger, impatience, or primitive reflexes have gotten the better of their partner. "Here, maybe I can help with this," is then viewed not as a threat to one person's parental power, but as a welcome intervention in a situation that was not going in the right direction. It also doesn't have to be seen by the child as a disagreement between parents about how to handle a situation, but rather as an example of the parents' collaborative skills. It all depends on how parents pull this off.

Perspective, of course, can go down the tubes as emotion mounts. It happens all the time that one parent will try to enlist their partner's assistance in an insupportable situation. "Can I get some support here?" an irate parent might say to his spouse who is contemplating her options because she feels his position is out of line. Sometimes just cutting to a time-out, for the kid and the angry parent, is the best way to defuse a circumstance without having to take sides. Taking immediate sides with the kid, after all, may just aggravate the other parent's frustration and heighten the child's uneasiness. Avoiding confrontation in the heat of the moment is not cowardly—unless violence is involved—but may be the shortest, most sedate distance to finding a solution or discussing the situation rationally. Kids with reasonable parents will learn sooner what they will inevitably learn later, that parents are not perfect and can be supportive of one another despite having healthy differences of opinion.

The best parenting tool to wield in dicey situations is a good sense of humor. A well-placed quip or self-deprecating comment can bring a tense situation to its knees in no time. A few weeks before the 1997 World Series was to begin, my husband came into the middle of one of the many speeches my son was habitually making in an effort to convince me to have the cable hooked up "just for a month." I was getting tired of the whole discussion. I was trying to arrange everyone's after-school schedules so there was enough time for homework, and I wasn't about to throw TV into the equation. Just before I threw up my hands and left the room, my husband interrupted the debate. "Hey," he deadpanned, "I forgot to tell you. I bought a 35-inch screen TV this afternoon. They were on sale and I thought to myself, what perfect timing." My jaw dropped and my blood pressure began to rise, then I saw him wink at my son. They both looked at me and grinned. "Gotcha," they said in unison.

Right then I knew it was time to take my thumb out of the dike and let the World Series flow. We could, given the pressure building up behind the TV debate, agree to agree on this subject—at least until the end of October.

Chapter Eight

Time Flies Whether You're Having Fun or Not

My parents . . . always told me I could do anything but never told me how long it would take.

—Rita Rudner

Time is fickle, but never more so than for busy women with children. It seems to pass differently depending on whether it is spent at work or at home, whether it is being contemplated by an adult or a child, or whether one looks back on it or into the future. And quality time, that wonderful space in each day that was going to make it possible to be both gainfully employed and a stellar mom, has turned out to be considerably less predictable than it was cracked up to be. All this means a mother must chart her own course as she allocates her time, remembering that children will draw their share only for a while. The time inevitably comes when children move on into their own lives, and a mother finds that her time is once again her own.

Carpe Diem

In our imperfect language, "time" is a word with many meanings, none of which accurately describe family time. In the work world, time is an orderly phenomenon. Lines on a workplace phone light up sequentially, designated lunch and coffee breaks punctuate the day, a person clocks in or out, meetings are scheduled to begin at one point and end at another, and, even in a fast-paced setting, when all is said and done you leave work and go home—to an entirely different time zone.

At home, where children spill food, wake up in the middle of the night, and throw up on things, time gets commandeered in myriad ways and can acquire a dreamlike quality wherein nothing ever quite gets done. Like interpreting a Salvador Dalí painting, time at home seems to have a different meaning depending on who interprets it. No beginning, middle, or end defines the work that needs doing. No predictable respite intervenes, sequence is elusive, and routine exists only as a target for disruption. The only thing that can be planned for with any certainty is the likelihood that things will seldom happen exactly the way they were envisioned.

The achievers in our midst seek to impose time management on this well-tested scenario. Adult education courses, business seminars, women-in-the-workplace conferences, continuing medical education forums—almost anywhere you look, you will find a course on how to manage your time more efficiently. Never mind that you have already squeezed time from the crevices of each day like water from a rock; someone is standing by to help you do it even better.

Heeding the time-management gurus, you document one child's schedule in pink in your day planner, another's in green, and yet another's in purple. For your appointments, you save the red and try not to mistake it for so many distress signals. You mount large flow charts on your kitchen wall to clarify who is to be where and when—always hoping the baby-sitter will show up and that you've gotten the details right. Memory lapses, car trouble, last-minute important phone calls—any little glitch—will throw everything off. Leaving a coach waiting in the dark with your kid will make you feel like a failure despite heroic efforts to manage that thing, that monster, called time.

Yet that monster, under most circumstances, is like income; the more you have the more you spend. Because most two-income couples are spending plenty of time on their respective careers before a single child arrives on the scene, they anticipate the relationship between parenting and time use as being comparable to retirement and money use. When it comes to parenting, the novice assumes that time can be managed, budgeted, and spent wisely. This is wishful thinking. Parenthood calls all nice and tidy assumptions into question, but perhaps never more decisively than when it comes to neat suppositions about time.

Every new round of parents also seems to insist, right up until they go from being DINKS (double-income, no kids) to moms and pops, that they are waiting for the "right" time to add a child to their already time-pressed lives. That right time, however, may be illusory, a mere quirk of perception. One couple I know waited several years for the right time to begin their family, then had their first child while they were smack dab in the middle of extensively remodeling their home, complete with no roof when it was raining, no hot water for long intervals, and television camera crews arriving early each morning to film segments of the work. Another couple put off becoming parents until four years after their marriage, then began the pregnancy while they were sailing in the South Seas. When they arrived back in the United States after a rough and dangerous Pacific crossing, the woman had lost fifteen pounds during her first trimester. Despite having chosen, their best intentions notwithstanding, what might sound like wrong times to become parents, both these couples went on to rise to the very occasions they probably would have avoided if a right time truly existed. They also began their families with great stories to tell their kids.

Time management, like the concept of a right time, is a figment of the business world, not the home front. Be it ever so humble, there is no place like home when it comes to time, perhaps because home is conspicuously plumbed with time sinks like television, telephone calls, home improvements, and the never-ending cycle of mess up and clean up.

Perhaps the trickiest part of reckoning time at work against time at home is that unlike the former, the latter tends to disappear in large chunks if you so much as blink. Our language needs one word to describe sixteen years of the same desk job, and quite another to describe the interval elapsed between when you first strap a toddler into a shopping cart and when you first hand her the car keys so she can do the shopping for you. Call it an instant, a time warp, or the twilight zone and try to keep it by ordinary means, but even Dalí's clocks won't keep time at home. The only way to "keep" time is to be on hand when the moment passes.

For Quality Time, Follow the Directions to Neverland

As men and women readily forged the two-income lifestyles on which they became immediately dependent, they both readily subscribed to the idea—the myth—of quality time. Quality time—a formative concept in the birth of Supermom as well as a certain contributor to her early demise—was one of the preeminent fallacies that created an entire generation of women who believed they were going to have and do "it" all at once. The idea that what really mattered to a child was the quality rather than the quantity of time a parent spent with the child was so convenient that it easily and instantly garnered a large and well-educated following.

I believed in this concept wholeheartedly and tried out the supposition any number of discouraging times before concluding that, together with other catchy but faulty phrases that litter the parenting landscape, the term "quality time" had never been test-driven by its etymological manufacturers. Together with phrases like "the perfect child," "marital bliss," "family values," and "sleep through the night," "quality time" was a misnomer that proved more of a hindrance than a help to parents pioneering their way through the career-kids-spouse maze. After realizing that time can't be qualified to make it magnetically appealing to a kid just because it is convenient for me, I felt like a kid who has just learned that Santa Claus doesn't exist, that I had just opened my parenting eyes for the first time to a large, shocking headline that read, "No, Virginia, There Is No Quality Time."

In reality, of course, this epiphany came much more slowly and painfully. I can't, or won't, remember all the occasions I convinced myself that quality could be sprinkled on time spent with one of my kids like so much fairy dust. Maybe the new understanding began with my internship, when my husband or nanny would bring my two-year-old daughter to the hospital to have dinner with me and I'd get summoned to the emergency room as soon as they arrived. Or maybe it was when I brought my second child home from the hospital and was going to do all the right things to encourage her older sister to love her, except that her older sister became terribly ill and had to be hospitalized for six days. Perhaps it was on a long-awaited family vacation, representing group quality time, when the one-hour plane trip turned into a nine-hour nightmare of landings and layovers and the long relaxing weekend in the country turned into a longer exhausting weekend catering to sequentially sick kids. The magic moments never materialized when they were supposed to.

This is not to say that special moments never occur. Any good parent-child relationship is built on a panoply of brief exchanges, long discussions, and shared experiences that accrue over time to form a unique bond. It doesn't take long, however, to discover that these episodes create you as a parent, you don't create them. Again during my internship, I'd come home after being on call and awake most of the night before, tired to the bone, and craving sleep. This was when my normal, rambunctious toddler wanted to play, a quality-time opportunity that depended on my ability to recognize and take advantage of it. As my children got older, those golden moments happened, not when I'd planned an afternoon off, but more often in the course of the mundane: when I was in the grocery store with a child, standing in line to check out a video, fixing dinner, driving to various after-school activities, or bandaging a wounded elbow. The accumulation of these small interactions lets me know how my children are doing and allows them to study how adults behave.

But treasured times are hard to orchestrate. My kids almost never respond to the question, "So, how was your day?" by holding forth for fifteen quality-time minutes on the things I most want to know about. The initial monosyllabic "Fine" is only elaborated on over the next several hours or days as things occur to the kids when they have too much food in their mouths at dinner or when they're asking me something about their homework. I'll be folding laundry, and one of my kids will show up to describe an episode at school; I'll be at my desk at 5:30 in the morning, and one of them will pad in with a book and ask me to read; I'll head toward the door with the dog, and one of them will tag along to share the sunset. More often than not, if I say, "Hey, let's go walk the dog and watch the sunset," they'll pass. Yet if the unspoken opportunity is there, sometimes so are they.

One of the reasons quality time sounded so appealing to women looking for ways to do too many things at once and feel good about it was that the concept was a product of an adult thought process. Children and adults, however, live on different planets where time is concerned. The twenty minutes until dinner is scarcely enough time for a parent to boil the spaghetti, but in kid minutes it's enough time to starve to death. With a month left before a birthday party, I feel like the walls are closing in fast, while that same month seems like an eternity to the kid waiting to age up. The three years left until my oldest goes off to college looks like a twinkling as I anticipate it, while to her it represents a full 20 percent of her life to date, not to mention three more years of high school.

Children view time altogether differently than do adults. If you've ever taken a nine-year-old son to the *Nutcracker* ballet, you may have had the rather uncomfortable experience of finding out that your idea of a good time doesn't jive with your son's. Or if you've ever had the heart wrench of watching your teenager become increasingly focused on everything but her family, you know that quality time doesn't increase, it diminishes as children grow. Children and adults have very different notions of how time passes and how to spend their time, which means these two very differently oriented individuals must find a common mood or purpose to allow even a moment of shared quality time.

Does this mean that parents must be slaves to kids' agendas or always be at attention to procure a sterling moment now and then? If this were the case, all parents—whether at home or at work—would be collective and colossal failures. No parent in the world can be on hand every time a child is ready to play or to pour his heart out, not anymore than a child will be at the ready whenever a parent wants to play. Yet somewhere amidst the din of schedules, somewhere between the time necessities, there needs to be a free time zone, an area into which a parent or child can wander and find the other one game for magical episodes that both will remember fondly later on.

Finding quality time is like trying to find Peter Pan's Neverland: "It might be miles beyond the moon, or right there where you stand. Just keep an open mind, and then suddenly you'll find, Never, Neverland." We shouldn't be surprised that, among the highlights of this mystical place, it is, "a place where dreams are born, and time is never planned."

But perhaps the most important clue Peter left, not only for Wendy but for all those attempting to be good mothers (whether to Lost Boys or not), was that Neverland, like quality time, is "not on any chart, you must find it with your heart," your heart in the right place at the right time.

Put Time on Your Side

The time crunch can, as much as if not more than other aspects of being married with children, create the feeling that no matter how hard you try you're always compromising in some area and no single endeavor ever gets your best efforts. As often happens in the course of rationing a scarce commodity, when you've served everyone else a portion of your time—a minute here, an hour there—you may have neglected to serve yourself a morsel of that time. You inevitably go to bed feeling deprived of exercise, entertainment, or even a few meditative moments, but because more time isn't likely to show up unexpectedly or an eighth day be added to each week, you understand that becoming resentful about the time shortage will only make matters worse.

A large and abiding concern exists among many mothers about how to find time for themselves. Sometimes this anxiety is justified. Every mother, for instance, needs time to exercise several times a week. On other occasions, however, this concern results from a self-centeredness that grew up with the "Me" generation and the pop culture. When a woman has exercised in the morning, worked all day, had lunch with her colleagues or friends, and still, because she comes home to the relentlessness of being married with children, complains that she can't seem to find any time for herself, there is something drastically wrong with the picture. If while simultaneously employed and raising a family you don't derive satisfaction from all sorts of small, even mundane pleasures each day, life is going to feel like a battle—one that you are chronically losing.

The three roles of wife, mother, and breadwinner consume most women with children. Other pursuits—such as hobbies, caretaking elderly parents, and volunteer work—also contribute to the balance of stress and bliss a woman maintains for herself, but because people do what they like doing best, it is important that each of these roles provide some sense of reward. In the absence of this fulfillment, any one role can become drudgery and diminish the enjoyment derived from the others. Once this downward spiral is set in motion, no amount of time away from what consumes your days will feel sufficient, and you will begin to feel like you need to get away, to find more and more time "for yourself." It's essential to recognize this state of mind and find ways to turn it around.

To address the daily march of time, I've become a habitual double dipper. This approach allows me to combine things I must do with things I like to do. For the last six years, for instance, I've coached my kids during soccer season, which serves a number of purposes at once. Several times a week I get to spend dedicated time with one child in the absence of her siblings, get my exercise for the day, nurture a hobby, give a little something back to the community in which I live, and have a blast doing it. On days when the house is a mess, the fridge is empty, a deadline is hovering, and I wish I didn't have to spend two hours coaching soccer, I consciously remind myself of what I get out of those two hours.

I stay current on medical topics or put a dent in my reading the same way. When the kids were quite small, I outfitted each of them with a small inexpensive tape player so they could listen to something like *Charlotte's Web* while I played a medical tape or book I wanted to hear on the car's cassette player. This way, whenever we had to spend a half-hour or more in the car, the kids were happily entertained, their minds off their stomachs and bladders, and I was able to chalk up either needed continuing medical education hours or plain old entertainment.

When, rarely, my husband and I have taken a long weekend away without the kids, we have usually combined business with pleasure to attend a medical conference. Similarly, when I'm at one of the kid's games or meets, I take the opportunity to stay in touch with other parents while enjoying the competition. At home, a cordless headset allows me to further maximize the two-birds-with-one-stone approach to time. I rarely talk on the phone, be it for business or pleasure, without doing something else at the same time. And exercise never stands alone. When I walk for exercise, the dog goes along for hers and I also get the day's news on my Walkman portable stereo. I never get on my stair stepper without a medical journal or other reading material. And so it goes. Given my existence's realities, waiting for a block of time to stretch out invitingly for a singular purpose would be like waiting for Godot, and equally frustrating.

The trick, where time is concerned, is to take the bull by its horns. You need to "govern the clock," as Golda Meir said and, "not be governed by it." You've got to find time, beat the clock, steal moments, and even "do" time in order to accomplish things you'd rather not think about. A mother's worst enemies are procrastination and avoidance, two deadly habits that will make an already imposing workload seem overwhelming or create an incessant feeling of failure. Time is best saved, not by the plethora of time-saving devices, some of which can ultimately cost time, but by steadily addressing the task that needs to be done and deriving the satisfaction that comes from having accomplished it.

I am the first to admit that this isn't always easy. Days when the domino effect has me running late to every encounter are stressful. It's easy to get discouraged when a line at the grocery store adds fifteen minutes to my plan to pick up one kid downtown, and the other daughter calls on the car phone from the opposite end of town, wondering why I'm not there yet even as I'm dashing down the freeway to get her. Being late picking up the first two means that getting to the midtown school to round up the two youngest on time is now hopeless. Rather than crawl out of my skin from frustration at every red light, I console myself that every kid is safe, and the worst that can happen is that I'll be charged for thirty minutes of after-school child care. Maintaining a buffer system of fallback positions is extremely helpful in keeping the stress dragon at bay.

Of all the roles a mother plays, the one that sooner or later occupies not only the most time but the most emotional space is that of parent. It may seem as though a woman has less control over the course of events in this role than in any other, a sense that can create discomfort for those who need to feel in control at all times. Precisely because of the roller-coaster nature of mothering, it's useful to identify the times, events, or projects that provide you the most enjoyment and try not to miss these. Conversely, it's useful to know what circumstances and time drains are recurrent sources of frustration.

To enjoy the good times and avoid the bad, it is essential to know your limits. Busy, ambitious, energetic women are prone to tackling too many things at once. When you've been asked to speak to a professional group and help organize a fund-raiser for your children's school the same week as one kid's slumber party and another kid's out-of-town baseball tournament, it's time to follow the same advice we've been giving kids for years and "just say no." If you find yourself always dreading a particular activity or event, stand back and figure out how to change or rearrange the circumstances. After years of carpools, for instance, I realized I was spending more time getting everyone else's kids around than if I just looked out for my own. As a result, I rarely participate in carpools—which may be just as well since my car is pretty full to begin with.

Being able to identify where satisfaction leaves off and frustration or a sense of being overwhelmed begins will serve more than your own interests. "When mama ain't happy, ain't nobody happy," according to a sign on a friend's refrigerator door. Knowing the truth in this can point the direction toward balance as clearly as any other indicator.

On any given weekend, for example, each of my children will have an athletic activity, a list of places they want to be taken, friends they want to invite over, and things they want me to do for them. I know as soon as the weekend begins to shape up on my calendar that if I'm planning to get a workout both days and a five-hour block of time at my computer, I'm going to be seriously disappointed. Instead, I'll exercise on Friday, sneak in a couple of hours of work early Saturday morning, then give the kids my full attention for the rest of the day. Saturday night or Sunday morning, I may squeeze in a couple more hours of work, and if I'm really lucky, I'll get in a workout on Sunday. If I didn't believe that most of the time I spend with my kids or my husband is "me" time, I'd be in big trouble. If I cringed each time one of my kids' agendas called to me, I'd be an unfit mother. If I felt constantly put upon by my children's needs instead of taking satisfaction from supporting them, I'd be miserable most of the time.

More than anything, the art of keeping several endeavors going at once—call it juggling or balancing, depending on how it feels—requires that you be able to sense when things are not going well and identify the point of friction. If your emotional radar picks up a frustration blip, its diffuse nature may seem overwhelming and difficult to contend with. But if you can narrow the aggravation down to something specific—having lost a whole day's work because your computer froze or having the kids and baby-sitter all sick at the same time—you won't be as inclined to dump your unhappiness everywhere you go and on everyone you meet.

In the midst of keeping many balls in the air, it's very important to know and respect your own limits and realize that these will change with your family's configuration and your career commitments. When I had two children not yet old enough to have multiple after-school activities, I volunteered many hours in wonderfully focused and productive ways and met good friends besides. Now that the soccer, swim, baseball, and basketball club teams all need money and volunteer hours, they have to get in line with the kids' three schools and other community causes for my time. It's tempting to sit in a meeting where a nongainfully employed mother who has one teenaged child is recruiting for help with her list of fund-raisers—one for every month of the year and this just for the swim team—and either have a panic attack or feel backed into an uncomfortable corner because I can't keep up with her agenda. To keep heart and soul together, however, I've learned to say yes to what I can do and feel good about, and no to everything else.

A sometimes not-so-obvious source of succor comes from reinforcing my professional information base. Just reading a good review article on hormone-replacement therapy, listening to a tape about common childhood illnesses, or finishing a book on children's behavioral issues can give my sense of well-being a shot in the arm. And of course, a good recreational read is better than psychotherapy.

Still, maintaining a blissful balance isn't always possible. A cranky husband, a surly teenager, a sick child, or a glitch at work can make everything seem impossible. Occasionally I come to one of these "poor me" junctions and know that, as surely as the kid who throws a golf ball at his sister needs a time out, I need one too. It need not be lengthy, maybe not even the recommended minute for every year of my age (which would get me a quick cup of coffee with a friend), but it needs to be a respite. Sometimes two minutes in the bathroom making faces at myself in the mirror is all it takes to make a smiling comeback. Other times it calls for a spontaneous dinner with my husband or a brief, solitary, restorative walk on the beach. Simple small pleasures now and then will provide the necessary fuel for positive daily progress.

202 IT'S NOT THE GLASS CEILING, IT'S THE STICKY FLOOR

Fly with Time, Not Against It

In our lifetime, we share ourselves here and there—sometimes more and sometimes less—with others. The years with children in the house demand a lot of us, but in the long run that time comes and goes like every other experience.

When my children were small, I couldn't envision an end to their time at home. Of necessity they had captured my heart and soul, and the thought that they would ever leave home and live apart from me was impossible to fathom. Even as one child gleefully hurled a jar of baby food from a shopping cart to watch it smash to smithereens and another scribbled in lipstick across the upholstery of the car, even as I dragged myself out of bed for the fourth time in a night or sprinted to pull the gushing hose out of the dining room, I knew that nothing could make this time with my children so uncomfortable that I would wish it away. Maybe, I thought secretly, they will stay forever. I didn't care about the messes.

Then in front of my eyes, albeit imperceptibly, each of these children grew into individuals—still my children, but not "mine" anymore. Each became his or her own person with interests beyond me. Soon my oldest will take the car keys in hand and no longer need me for transportation. Observing this process, watching this child take flight, is great validation for having invested what seemed like so much time while she was maturing, and wasn't so much time after all. I will miss her. I'll miss our daily talks in the car and the place she occupied in my thoughts when I knew she was waiting somewhere for me.

In some ways a parallel coming-of-age process looms simultaneously for my oldest daughter and me. While she is on the long, exhilarating runway that constitutes coming of age into adulthood, I will be coming of a different age. While she is beginning, I will be resuming. While she is setting out to determine who she is and what she wants to do, I will be getting back to the task of doing what I set out to do, even if it looks quite different now than it did before she was born. The nest, thanks to decades of feminism, will begin to fill as quickly as it empties.

For many years to come, my children will be piecing together what I've said and done with their own perceptions of how the world works and what it needs from them. No one grades a mother's work like her children do as they wend their way in the world. It's enough to make a mom want to scramble backward and pour more devotion, presence, and time onto the original effort. But, of course, those days (and years) are gone, moved aside by time in the interest of what happens next.

The trade-offs I've made for years begin to reverse themselves now. Rather than me handing my children increasing amounts of my time and pushing my professional commitments into ever more peripheral spheres as I have for fifteen years, they will, one by one, begin to return my time in bits and pieces, fits and starts, as they negotiate their way toward autonomy. Fortunately for mothers' hearts everywhere, this separation period is more gradual than a child's arrival. It is a transition at once as joyous and painful as the transitional phase of childbirth, but buffered by other children, continuing ties, and the knowledge that all the work that beckoned while the children were around more often is still there waiting for you. Another time is coming.